New Curriculum

Primary
Mathematics
Learn, practise and revise

Year 3

Anne Rainbow

Rising Stars UK Ltd, 7 Hatchers Mews, Bermondsey Street, London, SE1 3GS

www.risingstars-uk.com

Published 2013

Author: Anne Rainbow

Text design: Green Desert Ltd

Cover design: West 8 Design

Illustrations: Oxford Design and Illustrators

Publisher: Camilla Erskine

Editorial: Sparks (www.sparkspublishing.com)

British Library Cataloguing in Publication Data.

A CIP record for this book is available from the British Library.

ISBN: 978-0-85769-674-8

Printed by Craft Print International Ltd, Singapore

Contents

How to get the best out of this book

Each chapter spreads across two pages. All chapters focus on one topic and should help you to keep 'On track' and to 'Aim higher'.

Title: tells you the topic for the chapter.

What do you need to know? and **What will you learn?** tell you what you need to know before you start this chapter and what you are aiming to learn from this chapter.

Key facts: set out what you need to know and the ideas you need to understand fully.

Language: help to build up your mathematical vocabulary. Remember that some words mean one thing in everyday life and something more special in mathematics.

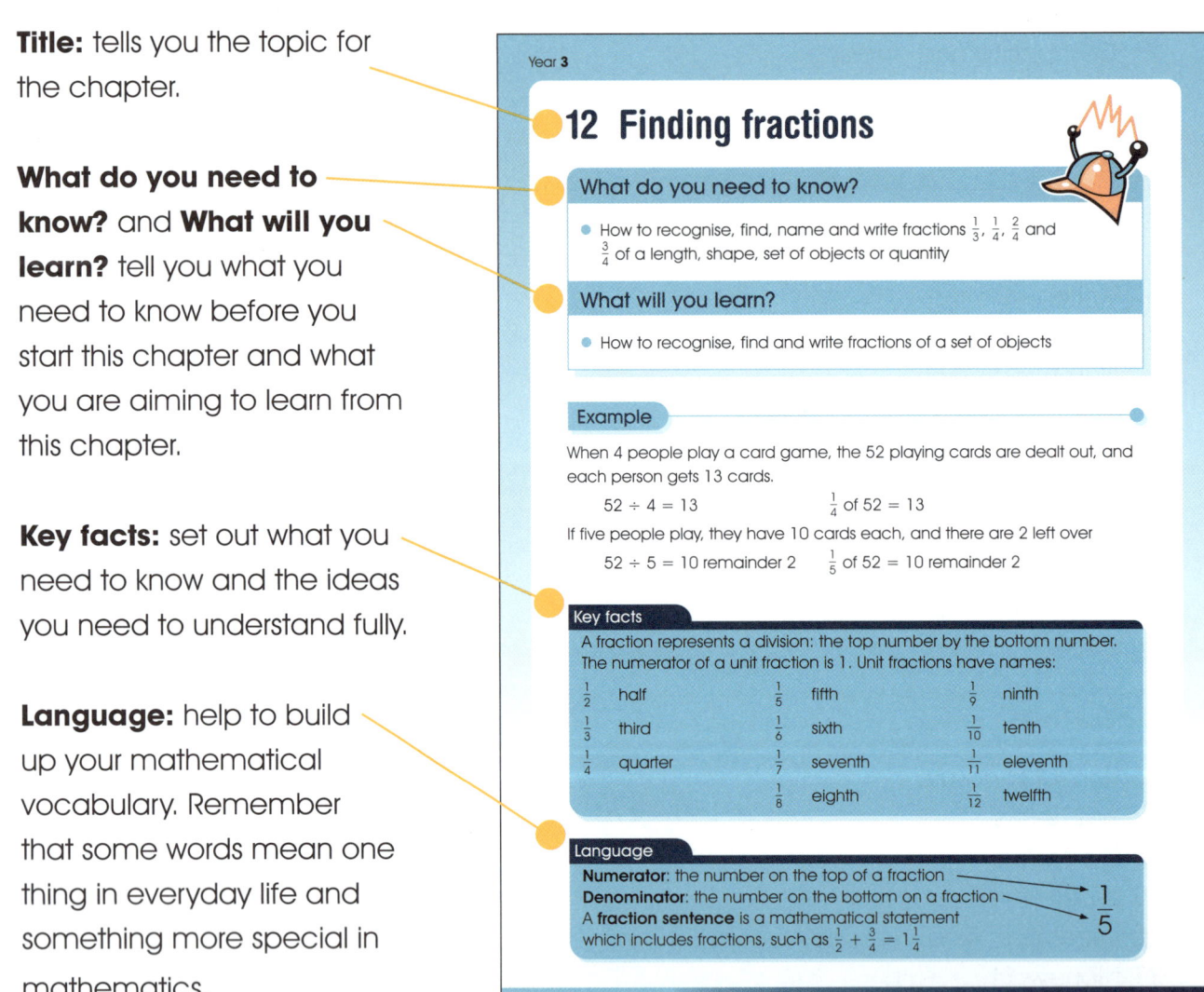

Year **3**

12 Finding fractions

What do you need to know?

- How to recognise, find, name and write fractions $\frac{1}{3}$, $\frac{1}{4}$, $\frac{2}{4}$ and $\frac{3}{4}$ of a length, shape, set of objects or quantity

What will you learn?

- How to recognise, find and write fractions of a set of objects

Example

When 4 people play a card game, the 52 playing cards are dealt out, and each person gets 13 cards.

$52 \div 4 = 13$ $\qquad$ $\frac{1}{4}$ of $52 = 13$

If five people play, they have 10 cards each, and there are 2 left over

$52 \div 5 = 10$ remainder 2 $\qquad$ $\frac{1}{5}$ of $52 = 10$ remainder 2

Key facts

A fraction represents a division: the top number by the bottom number. The numerator of a unit fraction is 1. Unit fractions have names:

$\frac{1}{2}$	half	$\frac{1}{5}$	fifth	$\frac{1}{9}$	ninth
$\frac{1}{3}$	third	$\frac{1}{6}$	sixth	$\frac{1}{10}$	tenth
$\frac{1}{4}$	quarter	$\frac{1}{7}$	seventh	$\frac{1}{11}$	eleventh
		$\frac{1}{8}$	eighth	$\frac{1}{12}$	twelfth

Language

Numerator: the number on the top of a fraction
Denominator: the number on the bottom on a fraction
A **fraction sentence** is a mathematical statement which includes fractions, such as $\frac{1}{2} + \frac{3}{4} = 1\frac{1}{4}$

$\frac{1}{5}$

28

Follow these simple rules if you are using the book for revising.

1 Read each page carefully. Give yourself time to take in each idea.

2 Learn the key facts and ideas. Ask your teacher or mum, dad or the adult who looks after you if you need help.

3 Concentrate on the things you find more difficult.

4 Only work for about 20 minutes at a time. Take a break and then do more work.

If you get most of the **On track** questions right then you know you are working at the expected level for the year. Well done – that's brilliant! If you get most of the **Aiming high** questions right, you are working at the top of expectations for your year. You're doing really well!

The **Using and applying questions** are often more challenging and ask you to explain your answers or think of different ways of answering. The questions give you the chance to use and apply your learning by answering mathematical problems.

The answers to all the questions are in the pull-out section in the middle of this book.

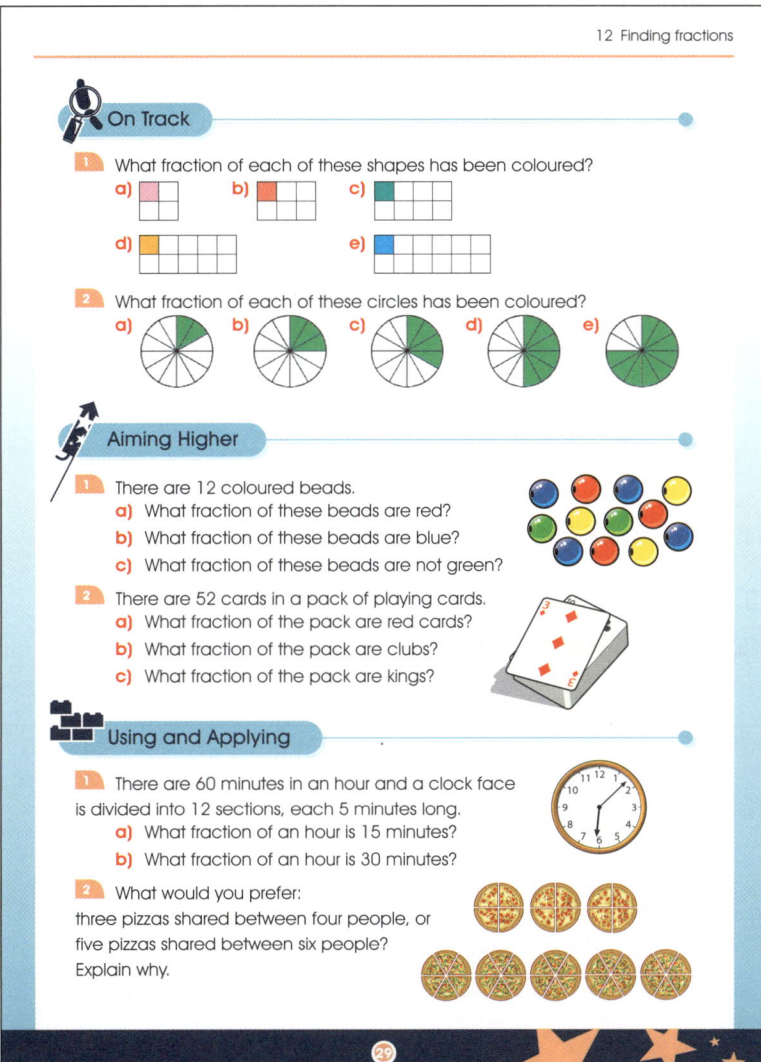

Follow these simple rules if you want to know how well you are doing.

1 Work through the questions.

2 Check your answers with your teacher or using the answer booklet in the middle of the book.

3 Keep a record of how well you do.

4 Write down anything you are finding difficult and work through the chapter again to see if you can find the answer. If you are still finding it hard, ask your teacher for help.

1 Numbers up to 1000

What do you need to know?

- What each digit in a 2-digit number stands for
- How to read and write numbers up to 100 in numerals and in words

What will you learn?

- What each digit in a 3-digit number stands for
- How to read and write numbers to at least 1000 in numerals and in words

Example

- Numbers can be written in numerals, using the digits 0–9, and in words.

  The number 999 is written as **nine hundred and ninety-nine**.
  The number 1000 is written as **one thousand**.

- In the number 45,
  the 4 represents 4 tens
  and the 5 represents 5 units.

  $$40 + 5 = 45$$

- In the number 392,
  the 3 represents 3 hundreds,
  the 9 represents 9 tens
  and the 2 represents 2 units.

  $$300 + 90 + 2 = 392$$

Key facts

The number after 99 is 100. The number after 999 is 1000.

Language

H = hundreds, T = tens, U = ones
2-digit number (TU): the first digit is the tens (T), the second digit is the units (U).
3 digit number (HTU): the first digit is the hundreds (H), the second digit is the Tens (T), the third digit is the units (U)

On Track

1. What does the number 4 represent in each of these numbers?
   a) 45   b) 64   c) 401   d) 143

2. Write these numbers using words.
   a) 271   b) 380   c) 426   d) 549

3. Write these numbers using numerals.
   a) one hundred and seventeen
   b) six hundred and ninety-five

Aiming Higher

1. With the digits 1, 6 and 8, you can make six different 3-digit numbers.

   168   186   618   681   816   861

   What does the digit 6 represent in each of these numbers?
   Write your answers in numerals and then in words.

2. Arrange the digits 2, 4 and 5 to make six different 3-digit numbers.
   What does the digit 5 represent in each of your numbers?
   Write your answers in numerals and then in words.

3. Arrange the digits 3, 7 and 9 to make two 3-digit numbers, each with the 9 representing 90. Write your answers in numerals and then in words.

Using and Applying

1. Write the number of your house in numerals and in words.
   Write the numbers of the houses one up and one down from your house, in numerals and in words.

2. The houses on Kate's side of Acacia Avenue have even numbers. Kate lives at number 134 and Lucy lives three doors down. What number house does Lucy live at? Write it in numerals and in words.

2 Comparing and ordering

What do you need to know?

- How to compare and order numbers from 0 to 100
- How to use <, > and = signs

What will you learn?

- How to compare numbers up to 1000
- How to order numbers up to 1000

Example

If two numbers are not equal, one is smaller and the other bigger.

For 1-digit numbers: $0 < 1 < 2 < 3 < 4 < 5 < 6 < 7 < 8 < 9$

For 2-digit numbers, look at the tens (T) column first.

$$\mathbf{2}2 < \mathbf{5}1 \quad \text{because} \quad 20 < 50$$

For 47 and 49, both with 4 in the T column:

$$4\mathbf{7} < 4\mathbf{9} \quad \text{because} \quad 7 < 9$$

For 3-digit numbers, look at the hundreds (H) column first.

$$\mathbf{3}91 < \mathbf{6}28 \quad \text{because} \quad 300 < 600$$

For 119 and 146, both with 1 in the H column:

$$1\mathbf{1}9 < 1\mathbf{4}6 \quad \text{because} \quad 10 < 40$$

For 572 and 576, both with 5 in the H column and 7 in the T column:

$$57\mathbf{2} < 57\mathbf{6} \quad \text{because} \quad 2 < 6$$

Key facts

When numbers are not equal, a **less than** symbol (<) or **greater than** symbol (>) can show which is smaller and which is bigger.
$22 < 51$ says the same as $51 > 22$.

Language

Putting numbers in order: writing them with the smallest first and the largest last, or the largest first and the smallest last.

On Track

1   Write two number sentences using 275 and 350 and < or >.

2   Write two number sentences using 841 and 609 and < or >.

3   Order these numbers, smallest first:

511   429   185   399   237

4   Order these numbers, largest first:

719   891   549   666   903

Aiming Higher

1   Order these numbers, largest first:

812   856   829   893   831

2   Order these numbers, smallest first:

973   935   957   975   735

Using and Applying

1   Find one number to fit these boxes which will make both these number sentences true.

   ☐ > 7   ☐ < 10

   How many other answers can you find?

2   List all the numbers which would fit these boxes and which will make both these number sentences true.

   ☐ > 56   ☐ < 61

3   In a game, children use a spinner to get a digit.
    Each player spins it two times.

    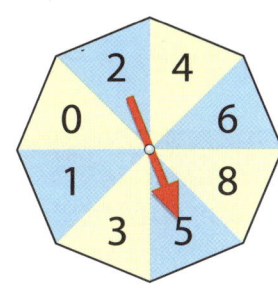

    a) What is the largest 2-digit whole number that could be made?

    b) What is the smallest 2-digit whole number that could be made?

3 Sequences

What do you need to know?

- How to count in steps of 2, 3 and 5
- How to count in 10s from any number, forward or backward

What will you learn?

- How to count in multiples of 4, 8, 50 and 100
- How to find 10 or 100 more or less than a given number

Example

Counting in steps of 10, only the T (tens) digit changes:

1	2	3	4	5	
11	12	13	14	15	
21	22	23	24	25	
31	32	33	34	35	
41	42	43	44	45	
51	52	53	54	55	

       4, 14, 24, 34, 44, 54, …

Counting in steps of 100, only the H (hundreds) digit changes:

       69, 169, 269, 369, 469, …

Counting in steps starting from zero gives the times tables of the value of the step:

Steps of 4:   0, 4, 8, 12, 16, …

Steps of 8:   0, 8, 16, 24, 32, …

Steps of 50:   0, 50, 100, 150, 200, …

Steps of 100:   0, 100, 200, 300, 400, …

Key facts

'Counting on' creates a sequence of numbers.

Language

A **sequence** is a list of numbers with a starting number and a rule that tells you how to work out all the numbers that follow it, for example, 'count on 4'.

 **On Track**

1 This sequence starts with 5 and the rule is 'count on 10'.
Write down the next four numbers.

5, 15, 25, ___, ___, ___, ___

2 This sequence starts with 17 and the rule is 'count on 100'.
Write down the next four numbers.

17, 117, 217, ___, ___, ___, ___

3 This sequence start with the number 0, and the rule is to 'count on 4'.
Write down the next four numbers.

0, 4, 8, 12, 16, ___, ___, ___, ___

 **Aiming Higher**

1 What number is 10 more than 74?
What number is 10 less than 74?

2 What number is 100 less than 523?
What number is 100 more than 523?

 **Using and Applying**

1 Amy is counting on in tens: 27, 37, 47, …
Carry on counting in tens until you go past 100.

2 Amy is counting back in hundreds: 854, 754, 654, …
Carry on counting in hundreds until you go past 100.

3 Anil and Bala are playing a counting-on game.
Anil counts up in eights and starts on zero.
Bala counts up in tens and starts on two.
They take it in turns to call out a number
in their sequence.
Anil starts first. Who was the first to say 32?
Show how you worked out your answer.

0, 8, 16, …   2, 12, …

4 Mental addition

What do you need to know?

- Addition facts to 20
- How to add mentally: a 2-digit number and ones or tens, two 2-digit numbers and three 1-digit numbers

What will you learn?

- How to add mentally: a 3-digit number and ones or tens or hundreds

Example

To add ones to a 3-digit number, e.g. for 72**5** + **6**,

remember that $5 + 6 = 11$

so $2\textbf{5} + \textbf{6} = 31$

and $72\textbf{5} + \textbf{6} = 731$

To add tens to a 3-digit number, e.g. 4**31** + **5**0, the units won't change.

Use an addition fact for the tens column:

$3 + 5 = 8$ $30 + 50 = 80$

                                        $4\textbf{31} + \textbf{5}0 = 4\textbf{81}$

When adding hundreds, only the hundreds column is changed:

$\textbf{3}13 + \textbf{200} = \textbf{5}13$ $\textbf{3}13 + \textbf{400} = \textbf{7}13$

Key facts

The order in which you add numbers does not matter: $3 + 5 = 5 + 3$
To add hundreds to a 3-digit number, count on in hundreds, remembering that only the H (hundreds) digit will change.
    313, 413, 513, …

Language

Partition: to split a number into Ts and Us, like $36 = 30 + 6$, or in some other way to help you to do a calculation, like $36 = 20 + 16$.
Count on: add a number.

 **On Track**

1 Do these sums in your head.
a) 2 + 4 + 7   b) 9 + 2 + 8   c) 8 + 5 + 1   d) 7 + 1 + 5

2 Do these sums in your head.
a) 94 + 7   b) 96 + 9   c) 95 + 8   d) 97 + 6

3 Do these sums in your head.
a) 74 + 40   b) 69 + 70   c) 81 + 60   d) 32 + 90

4 Do these sums in your head.
a) 54 + 52   b) 76 + 61   c) 44 + 71   d) 83 + 56

 **Aiming Higher**

1 Do these sums in your head.
a) 614 + 7   b) 406 + 9   c) 915 + 5   d) 711 + 6

2 Do these sums in your head.
a) 544 + 30   b) 161 + 70   c) 440 + 80   d) 839 + 90

3 Do these sums in your head.
a) 514 + 200   b) 169 + 700   c) 381 + 300   d) 232 + 500

 **Using and Applying**

1 In this number square, the sum of the first two cells in each row equals the number in the third cell.

The same is true for the columns.
Use addition facts to complete the square.

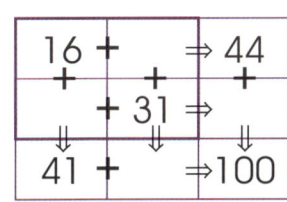

2 Make up your own square with a corner number of 100.

3 Make up your own square with a corner number of 1000.

5 Mental subtraction

What do you need to know?

- Addition and subtraction facts to 20
- How to add and subtract mentally: a 2-digit number and ones or tens
- How to add and subtract mentally: two 2-digit numbers
- How to add and subtract mentally: three 1-digit numbers

What will you learn?

- How to subtract mentally: a 3-digit number and ones or tens or hundreds

Example

To subtract ones from a 3-digit number, imagine a number line and count back.

| | | | | | |
|344|345|346|347|348|349|

For 347 – 2, start at 347 and count back 2.   347 – 2 = 345

For 348 – 4, start at 348 and count back 4.   348 – 4 = 344

To subtract tens from a 3-digit number   792 – **6**0
you could use a subtraction fact: 9 – 6 = 3   90 – 60 = 30
                                                 792 – **6**0 = 7**3**2

To subtract hundreds, only the hundreds column is changed:

$$415 - 200 = 215$$

Key facts

Subtraction: the order does matter! $3 - 2 \neq 2 - 3$

Language

Partition: to write a number another way, e.g. 432 = 420 + 12
Count back: subtract a number

On Track

1 Do these calculations in your head.
a) 12 – 4 – 7   b) 19 – 2 – 8   c) 18 – 5 – 1   d) 17 – 1 – 5

2 Do these calculations in your head.
a) 94 – 7   b) 96 – 9   c) 95 – 8   d) 97 – 6

3 Do these calculations in your head.
a) 74 – 40   b) 69 – 20   c) 81 – 60   d) 92 – 50

4 Do these calculations in your head.
a) 64 – 52   b) 76 – 61   c) 84 – 71   d) 83 – 56

Aiming Higher

1 Do these calculations in your head.
a) 614 – 70   b) 406 – 90   c) 915 – 50   d) 711 – 60

2 Do these calculations in your head.
a) 544 – 30   b) 161 – 70   c) 440 – 80   d) 839 – 90

3 Do these calculations in your head.
a) 514 – 200   b) 869 – 700   c) 381 – 300   d) 932 – 500

Using and Applying

1 There are 168 children on a school trip. 70 are boys.
How many of them are girls? Explain how you know.

2 In Year 3, there are 119 children. There are 60 boys in Year 3.
How many girls are there? Explain how you know.

3 Use these four number cards and the subtraction card to make a
calculation whose answer is 22.

3      5      –

6 Written addition

What do you need to know?

- How to record, in writing, the addition of two 2-digit numbers
- That addition can be done in any order: $56 + 17 = 17 + 56$

What will you learn?

- How to record, in writing, the addition of two 3-digit numbers

Example

```
H T U
1 3 5
2 4 2 +
-------
3 7 7
```

$1 + 2 < 10$

$3 + 4 < 10$

$5 + 2 < 10$ There is no need to carry.

In the U column,
$5 + 9 = 14 > 10$.

The 4 is written in the U column.
The 10 is carried as a 1 into the
T column

```
H T U
1 3 5
2 4 9 +
-------
3 8 4
    1
```

The 'carry 1' can be written below the bottom answer line, or above the top answer line.

```
H T U
1 3 5
2 4 9 +
  1
-------
3 8 4
```

Key facts

The value of a digit depends on its position, so it is important to line up the columns carefully.

Language

H stands for hundreds. **T** stands for tens. **U** stands for units.
Carry 1: when ten 1s from the U column are carried as a 1 into the T column (or when ten 10s from the T column are carried as a 1 into the H column).

 **On Track**

1 Do these sums, showing your working.
   a) 57 + 36 **b)** 49 + 28 **c)** 35 + 18 **d)** 64 + 27

2 Do these sums, showing your working.
   a) 82 + 39 **b)** 68 + 44 **c)** 77 + 55 **d)** 93 + 18

3 Do these sums, showing your working.
   a) 137 + 46 **b)** 328 + 27 **c)** 719 + 45 **d)** 582 + 19

 **Aiming Higher**

1 Do these sums, showing your working.
   a) 597 + 361 **b)** 392 + 271 **c)** 635 + 182 **d)** 864 + 271

2 Do these sums, showing your working.
   a) 628 + 194 **b)** 468 + 145 **c)** 757 + 165 **d)** 493 + 189

 **Using and Applying**

1 The teacher has marked Katie's sums as wrong.

a) 145	b) 782	c) 396
238 +	127 +	144 +
473 ✗	809 ✗	252 ✗

Check the workings to find Katie's mistakes. Explain how you know.
Re-do the sums correctly.

2 Compare your answers to all the sums on this page with someone else's. If you disagree on an answer, check both sums and see where the mistake has been made. Explain how you know.

7 Written subtraction

What do you need to know?

- How to record, in writing, the subtraction of one 2-digit number from another 2-digit number
- That the order matters when subtraction: $56 - 17 \neq 17 - 56$

What will you learn?

- How to record, in writing, the subtracting of one 3-digit number from another 3-digit number

Example

$7 > 2, 8 > 4$ and $5 > 2$ so no need to borrow.

In the U column, $6 < 9$ so 'borrow' a 10 from the 50. $56 = 40 + 16$

Cross through the 5 and write a small 4 in its place.
Write a small 1 next to the 6.
$16 - 9 = 7$. Put 7 in the U column.
$4 - 1 = 3$. Put 3 in the T column.
$8 - 2 = 6$. Put 6 in the H column.

```
H T U
7 8 5
2 4 2 −
───────
5 4 3
```

```
H T U
8 5 6
2 1 9 −
───────
      ?
```

```
H T U
8 4⁄5 ¹6
2 1 9 −
───────
    3 7
```

```
H T U
8 4⁄5 ¹6
2 1 9 −
───────
  6 3 7
```

Key facts

The value of a digit depends on its position within a number, so it is important to line up the columns carefully.

Language

H stands for hundreds. **T** stands for tens. **U** stands for units.
Borrowing: when 1 in the T column is changed into ten 1s for the U column, or when a 1 in the H column is changed into ten 10s for the T column

On Track

1 Do these calculations, showing your working.
a) 57 – 36 **b)** 79 – 23 **c)** 39 – 12 **d)** 68 – 27

2 Do these calculations, showing your working.
a) 382 – 131 **b)** 467 – 244 **c)** 577 – 252 **d)** 693 – 441

3 Do these calculations, showing your working.
a) 482 – 138 **b)** 362 – 214 **c)** 673 – 255 **d)** 793 – 446

Aiming Higher

1 Do these calculations, showing your working.
a) 527 – 363 **b)** 718 – 271 **c)** 635 – 182 **d)** 864 – 271

2 Do these calculations, showing your working.
a) 621 – 194 **b)** 412 – 145 **c)** 753 – 165 **d)** 413 – 189

Using and Applying

1 The teacher has marked Katie's sums as wrong.

a) 645	b) 782	c) 396
238 –	127 –	144 –
413 ✗	665 ✗	540 ✗

Check the workings to find Katie's mistakes. Explain how you know.
Re-do the sums, correctly.

2 Compare your answers to all the sums on this page with someone else's. If you disagree on an answer, check both sums and see where the mistake has been made. Explain how you know.

8 Number problems

What do you need to know?

- How to solve simple one-step problems with addition and subtraction
- How to use the inverse relationship between addition and subtraction to check answers

What will you learn?

- How use number facts and place value to solve problems
- How to solve more complex problems, including missing number problems

Example

Problems are written using words.

The problem tells you which numbers to use: 200, 300 and 500.

A cinema has three screens, seating 200, 300 and 500 people. What is the total number of seats?

'Total' tells you to add up the numbers.

Do the sum …

$200 + 300 + 500 = 1000$

In total, there are 1000 seats.

… but write your answer as a sentence.

Key facts

All the information you need is written in the question. Read it carefully.
To be double sure, read it twice, or even three times.
A **?** is often used in place of a missing number.

Language

Problem solving: working out what to do to find the answer

On Track

1 What are the missing numbers?
  a) 100 – ? = 43   **b)** 100 – ? = 27
  c) 100 – ? = 56   **d)** 100 – ? = 32

Write an addition fact that helped you to work out each answer.

2 What are the missing numbers?
  a) 154 – ? = 40   **b)** 293 – ? = 60
  c) 482 – ? = 50   **d)** 381 – ? = 30

Write an addition fact that helped you to work out each answer.

3 What are the missing numbers?
  a) 211 + ? = 240   **b)** 123 + ? = 160
  c) 437 + ? = 480   **d)** 251 + ? = 300

Write a subtraction fact that helped you to work out each answer.

Aiming Higher

1 Jim has 42 marbles and Ali has 37 marbles.
  a) How many marbles do they have altogether?
  b) How many more marbles than Ali does Jim have?
  c) Explain how you solved parts a) and b).

2 Sam had 50 pies. He sold some and then had 17 left. How many pies did Sam sell? Explain how you solved this problem.

Using and Applying

1 Make up a word problem that can be solved using this addition fact:
47 + 53 = 100

2 Make up a word problem that can be solved using this subtraction fact: 144 – 96 = 48

9 Multiplication and division facts

What do you need to know?

- Multiplication and division facts for the 2, 5 and 10 multiplication tables and how to write facts using $\times$, $\div$ and $=$
- How to recognise odd and even numbers

What will you learn?

- Multiplication and division facts for the 3, 4 and 8 multiplication tables

Example

For each multiplication fact there are two division facts.

- You should know your 2, 5 and 10 times tables.

$5 \times 6 = 30$
$30 \div 5 = 6$
$30 \div 6 = 5$

	1	2	3	4	5	6	7	8	9	10
2	2	4	6	8	10	12	14	16	18	20
5	5	10	15	20	25	30	35	40	45	50
10	10	20	30	40	50	60	70	80	90	100

- The same is true for the 3, 4 and 8 times tables.

$4 \times 6 = 24$
$24 \div 4 = 6$
$24 \div 6 = 4$

	1	2	3	4	5	6	7	8	9	10
3	3	6	9	12	15	18	21	24	27	30
4	4	8	12	16	20	24	28	32	36	40
8	8	16	24	32	40	48	56	64	72	80

Key facts

The order does not matter with multiplication: $5 \times 6 = 6 \times 5 = 30$
Order does matter with division $30 \div 5 \neq 5 \div 30$

Language

30 is a **multiple** of 5 and 30 is a **multiple** of 6.
For each **multiplication fact** such as $5 \times 6 = 30$, there are two
matching **division facts**: $30 \div 5 = 6$ and $30 \div 6 = 5$.

On Track

1 You should now know your 3, 4 and 8 times tables.
Try to do these from memory.

a) 3×4 **b)** 3×8 **c)** 4×8 **d)** 8×4

e) 3×6 **f)** 4×7 **g)** 6×8 **h)** 8×9

i) 3×7 **j)** 4×9 **k)** 5×8 **l)** 7×8

2 Which of the answers to question 1 are even?
Explain how you know.

Aiming Higher

1 Try to do these from memory.
a) $32 \div 4$ **b)** $56 \div 8$ **c)** $27 \div 3$ **d)** $24 \div 6$

2 $3 \times 9 = 27$ so $27 \div 9 = 3$ and $27 \div 3 = 9$. For each of these multiplication facts, write two division facts.
a) $4 \times 6 = 24$ **b)** $3 \times 5 = 15$ **c)** $2 \times 8 = 16$ **d)** $5 \times 4 = 20$

3 How many different division facts can you write for each of these multiplication facts?
a) $3 \times 3 = 9$ **b)** $4 \times 4 = 16$ **c)** $5 \times 5 = 25$ **d)** $8 \times 8 = 64$

Explain your answer.

Using and Applying

1 I am thinking of a number between 20 and 35. It is a multiple of 3 and a multiple of 4. What is my number?

2 I am thinking of a number between 15 and 40. It is a multiple of 3 and a multiple of 4. What numbers could it be?

3 I am thinking of a number between 40 and 80. It is a multiple of 3 and a multiple of 8. What numbers could it be? Compare your answer with a friend. Did you both find the same answers?

4 Make up a number puzzle of your own and test it on a friend.

10 Multiplication and division

What do you need to know?

- The times tables for 2, 3, 4, 5, 8 and 10
- What each digit in a 3-digit number stands for: its place value

What will you learn?

- Written methods for multiplication and division of 2-digit numbers by 1-digit numbers

Example

- You can show 3 × 8 as an array of squares and count the squares.

3 rows

1	2	3	4	5	6	7	8
9	10	11	12	13	14	15	16
17	18	19	20	21	22	23	**24**

8 columns

3 × 8 = 24

You can also use the same array to work out a division. 24 ÷ 3 = 8

- For larger numbers, you might use a multiplication grid.

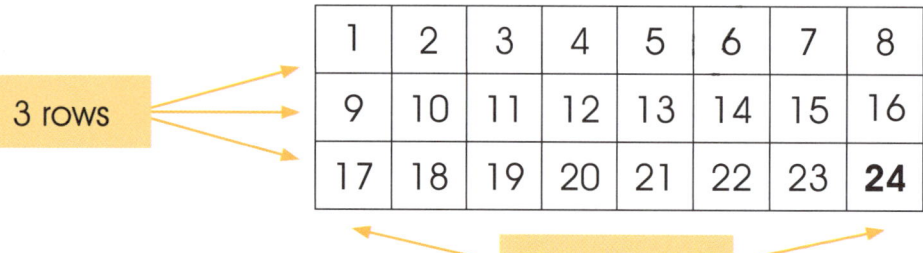

×	10	3	13
4	40	12	**52**

So, to find 13 × 4 add 40 and 12

13 = 10 + 3 and your 4 times table tells you 10 × 4 and 3 × 4

Key facts

Multiplication sums can be shown as an array.
Number of rows × number of columns = Number within the array

Language

An **array** is a rectangular arrangement.
Place value: the value of a digit due to its position within a number

On Track

1 For each of these multiplications, draw an array to find the answer.
  a) 4×7 **b)** 9×4 **c)** 7×6 **d)** 7×8

2 For these divisions, draw an array to find each answer.
  a) $32 \div 8$ **b)** $48 \div 8$ **c)** $64 \div 8$ **d)** $72 \div 8$

Aiming Higher

1 Do these multiplications. Show your workings.
  a) 81×4 **b)** 62×5 **c)** 63×8 **d)** 64×3
  e) 34×7 **f)** 85×3 **g)** 42×8 **h)** 57×5

2 Do these divisions. Show your workings.
  a) $63 \div 3$ **b)** $64 \div 4$ **c)** $72 \div 3$ **d)** $76 \div 4$
  e) $88 \div 4$ **f)** $88 \div 8$ **g)** $96 \div 4$ **h)** $95 \div 5$

Using and Applying

1 Egg trays have 4 rows and 6 columns.
On Monday, your hens lay 21 eggs.
Imagine putting these into an egg tray.

  a) How many rows of eggs can be filled?

  b) How many eggs will be in the partly filled row?

2 Egg boxes each hold six eggs.
On Tuesday, the hens lay 18 eggs.
How many egg boxes will you need for
Tuesday's eggs?

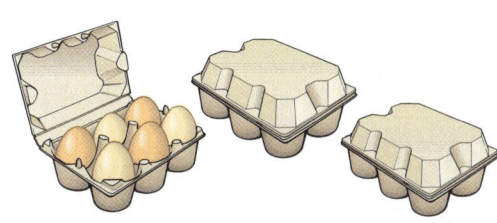

3 On Wednesday, the hens lay 19 eggs. How many egg boxes will you
need? Explain your answer.

11 More number problems

What do you need to know?

- How to use multiply and divide to solve one-step problems with multiplication and division

What will you learn?

- How to solve more complex problems involving multiplication and division
- How to solve missing number problems

Example

Problems are written using words and these words tell you the operation to use. For example, 'share' tells you to divide.

Question: Gerry has three different shirts and two different pairs of jeans. How many different outfits does he have?

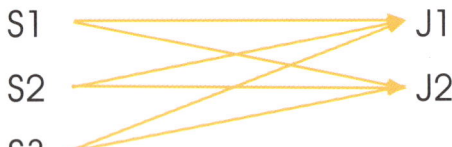

> 'How many different' tells you to multiply.
> $3 \times 2 = 6$

Using a question mark can help when solving a missing number problem.

I am thinking of a number.	Use ? for the number.
I multiply it by 10 and add 30. I get 430.	$? \times 10 + 30 = 430$
What was my number?	$? \times 10 = 430 - 30 = 400$
	$? = 40$

Key facts

A **?** is often used in place of a missing number.

Language

Problem solving: understanding the problem, then deciding on a strategy, doing the calculations and then checking your working

On Track

1   Solve these problems and show your working. How did you know which operation to use?

   a) What number is five more than seventeen?

   b) What number is sixteen less than forty?

2   Solve these problems and show your working. How did you know which operation to use?

   a) What number is double seventeen?

   b) What number is half of seventy-two?

Aiming Higher

1   I am thinking of an even number between 10 and 20. I add 7 and get 19. What is my number?

2   I am thinking of an odd number between 20 and 30. I subtract 5 and get 18. What is my number?

3   I am thinking of a number and double it. I add 3 and get 19. What is my number?

4   Make up your own number puzzle and try it out on a friend.

Using and Applying

1   In a card game, the pack of 52 cards is dealt out to four players. How many cards does each player have in their hand?

2   A recipe for 6 small cakes requires 1 egg and 65g each of butter, caster sugar and self-raising flour. To make 12 cakes, what ingredients are needed?

3   Priya has 3 different hats and 4 different coats. How many different outfits does she have?

12 Finding fractions

What do you need to know?

- How to recognise, find, name and write fractions $\frac{1}{3}$, $\frac{1}{4}$, $\frac{2}{4}$ and $\frac{3}{4}$ of a length, shape, set of objects or quantity

What will you learn?

- How to recognise, find and write fractions of a set of objects

Example

When 4 people play a card game, the 52 playing cards are dealt out, and each person gets 13 cards.

$$52 \div 4 = 13 \qquad\qquad \frac{1}{4} \text{ of } 52 = 13$$

If five people play, they have 10 cards each, and there are 2 left over

$$52 \div 5 = 10 \text{ remainder } 2 \qquad \frac{1}{5} \text{ of } 52 = 10 \text{ remainder } 2$$

Key facts

A fraction represents a division: the top number by the bottom number. The numerator of a unit fraction is 1. Unit fractions have names:

$\frac{1}{2}$	half	$\frac{1}{5}$	fifth	$\frac{1}{9}$	ninth
$\frac{1}{3}$	third	$\frac{1}{6}$	sixth	$\frac{1}{10}$	tenth
$\frac{1}{4}$	quarter	$\frac{1}{7}$	seventh	$\frac{1}{11}$	eleventh
		$\frac{1}{8}$	eighth	$\frac{1}{12}$	twelfth

Language

Numerator: the number on the top of a fraction

Denominator: the number on the bottom on a fraction

A **fraction sentence** is a mathematical statement which includes fractions, such as $\frac{1}{2} + \frac{3}{4} = 1\frac{1}{4}$

$$\frac{1}{5}$$

On Track

1 What fraction of each of these shapes has been coloured?

a)    b) 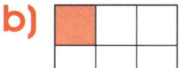   c)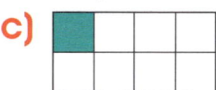

d) 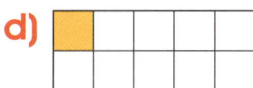   e)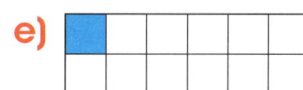

2 What fraction of each of these circles has been coloured?

a)    b)    c)    d) 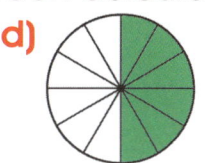   e)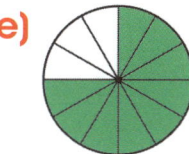

Aiming Higher

1 There are 12 coloured beads.
   a) What fraction of these beads are red?
   b) What fraction of these beads are blue?
   c) What fraction of these beads are not green?

2 There are 52 cards in a pack of playing cards.
   a) What fraction of the pack are red cards?
   b) What fraction of the pack are clubs?
   c) What fraction of the pack are kings?

Using and Applying

1 There are 60 minutes in an hour and a clock face is divided into 12 sections, each 5 minutes long.
   a) What fraction of an hour is 15 minutes?
   b) What fraction of an hour is 30 minutes?

2 What would you prefer:
three pizzas shared between four people, or
five pizzas shared between six people?
Explain why.

13 Comparing and ordering fractions

What do you need to know?

- That $\frac{2}{4} = \frac{1}{2}$

What will you learn?

- How to compare and order fractions

Example

With unit fractions, as the denominator gets bigger, the fraction gets smaller:

$$\frac{1}{2} > \frac{1}{4} > \frac{1}{6} > \frac{1}{8} > \frac{1}{10} > \frac{1}{12}$$

As the numerator increases, fractions with the same denominator get bigger:

$$\frac{1}{12} < \frac{3}{12} \qquad \frac{5}{12} < \frac{7}{12} \qquad \frac{9}{12} < \frac{11}{12}$$

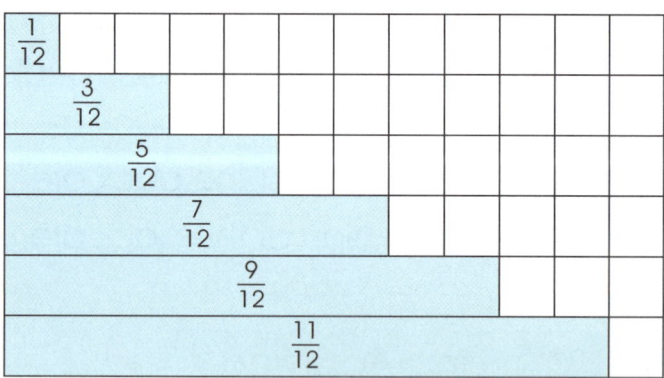

Key facts

When the top and the bottom number are the same, the result of the division is 1.

$$1 = \frac{2}{2} = \frac{3}{3} = \frac{4}{4}$$

Language

< stands for 'less than'. > stands for 'greater than'.

A **fraction sentence** is a mathematical statement which includes fractions, such as $\frac{1}{2} + \frac{3}{4} = 1\frac{1}{4}$

 **On Track**

1 Write a fraction sentence for this diagram.

$\frac{1}{3}$ $\frac{2}{3}$

2 Write fraction sentences for these diagrams.

a) 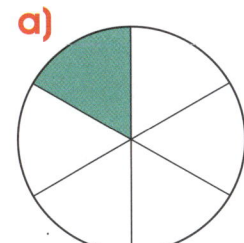 **b)** 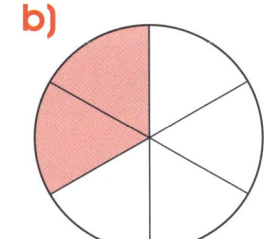 **c)**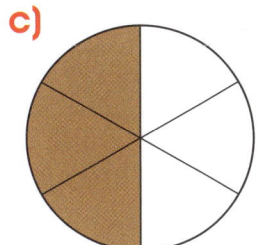

Aiming Higher

1 Put these fractions in order, from smallest to largest.

$\frac{1}{12}$ $\frac{1}{9}$ $\frac{1}{2}$ $\frac{1}{7}$ $\frac{1}{3}$

2 Put these fractions in order, from largest to smallest.

$\frac{2}{9}$ $\frac{5}{9}$ $\frac{1}{9}$ $\frac{7}{9}$ $\frac{8}{9}$

3 Put these fractions in order, from smallest to largest.

$\frac{5}{6}$ $\frac{3}{4}$ $\frac{1}{2}$ $\frac{7}{12}$ $\frac{1}{4}$

Explain your answer by drawing shaded diagrams.

 **Using and Applying**

1 I am thinking of three fractions that add up to 1. One of them is $\frac{1}{4}$. What might the other two fractions be?

2 I am thinking of three fractions that add up to 1. The first fraction is one-half of the second fraction and one-third of the third fraction. What are my three fractions?

14 Calculations with fractions

What do you need to know?

- That a fraction represents a division: the top number by the bottom number.

What will you learn?

- How to add and subtract fractions with the same denominator within one whole (e.g. $\frac{5}{7} + \frac{1}{7} = \frac{6}{7}$)

Example

Here is a bar of chocolate.

It is marked into 12 squares, and each square is one-twelfth of the bar.

If you eat 1 square and then another square, how much of the bar have you eaten?

$\frac{1}{12} + \frac{1}{12} = \frac{2}{12}$

How much of the bar is left?

$\frac{12}{12} - \frac{2}{12} = \frac{10}{12}$

Notice that $\frac{2}{12} = \frac{1}{6}$

Notice that $\frac{10}{12} = \frac{5}{6}$

Key facts

To add two fractions, they first need to have the same denominator.

$\frac{1}{12} + \frac{10}{12} = \frac{11}{12}$

Language

Numerator: the number on the top of a fraction

Denominator: the number on the bottom on a fraction

A **fraction sentence** is a mathematical statement that includes fractions, such as $\frac{3}{7} + \frac{2}{7} = \frac{5}{7}$

$\frac{3}{7}$

Mathematics Study Guide: Year 3

Answer Booklet

Unit 1 Numbers up to 1000
On track
1 a) 40
  b) 4
  c) 400
  d) 40
2 a) two hundred and seventy-one
  b) three hundred and eighty
  c) four hundred and twenty-six
  d) five hundred and forty-nine
3 a) 117
  b) 695
Aiming higher
1 168, 60, sixty; 186, 6, six; 618, 600, six hundred; 681, 600, six hundred; 816, 6, six; 861, 60, sixty
2 245, 5, five; 254, 50, fifty; 425, 5, five; 452, 50, fifty; 524, 500, five hundred; 542, 500, five hundred
3 397, three hundred and ninety-seven; 793, seven hundred and ninety-three
Using and applying
1 N/A
2 128, one hundred and twenty-eight

Unit 2 Comparing and ordering
On track
1 275 < 350 and 350 > 275
2 841 > 609 and 609 < 841
3 185, 237, 399, 429, 511
4 903, 891, 719, 666, 549
Aiming higher
1 893, 856, 831, 829, 812
2 735, 935, 957, 973, 975
Using and applying
1 8, 9
2 57, 58, 59, 60
3 a) 88   b) 10

Unit 3 Sequences
On track
1 35, 45, 55, 65
2 317, 417, 517, 617
3 20, 24, 28, 32
Aiming higher
1 84, 64
2 423, 623
Using and applying
1 57, 67, 77, 87, 97, 107
2 554, 454, 354, 254, 154, 54
3 Bala says 32 first. Anil: 0, 8, 16, 24, 32, Bala: 2, 12, 22, 32, …

Unit 4 Mental addition
On track
1 a) 13   b) 19
  c) 14   d) 13
2 a) 101   b) 105
  c) 103   d) 103
3 a) 114   b) 139
  c) 141   d) 122
4 a) 106   b) 137
  c) 115   d) 139
Aiming higher
1 a) 621   b) 415
  c) 920   d) 717

2 a) 574   b) 231
  c) 520   d) 929
3 a) 714   b) 869
  c) 681   d) 732
Using and applying
1

16	28	44
25	31	56
41	59	100

2 N/A
3 N/A

Unit 5 Mental subtraction
On track
1 a) 1   b) 9
  c) 12   d) 11
2 a) 87   b) 87
  c) 87   d) 91
3 a) 34   b) 49
  c) 21   d) 42
4 a) 12   b) 15
  c) 13   d) 27
Aiming higher
1 a) 544   b) 316
  c) 865   d) 651
2 a) 514   b) 91
  c) 360   d) 749
3 a) 314   b) 169
  c) 81   d) 432
Using and applying
1 98 girls
2 59 girls
3 56 – 34 = 22; 65 – 43 = 22

Unit 6 Written addition
On track
1 a) 93   b) 77
  c) 53   d) 91
2 a) 121   b) 112
  c) 132   d) 111
3 a) 183   b) 355
  c) 764   d) 601
Aiming higher
1 a) 958   b) 663
  c) 817   d) 1135
2 a) 822   b) 613
  c) 922   d) 682
Using and applying
1 a) 383
  b) 909
  c) 540
2 N/A

Unit 7 Written subtraction
On track
1 a) 21   b) 56
  c) 27   d) 41
2 a) 251   b) 223
  c) 325   d) 252
3 a) 344   b) 148
  c) 418   d) 347
Aiming higher
1 a) 164   b) 447
  c) 453   d) 593

2 a) 427   b) 267
  c) 588   d) 224
Using and applying
1 a) 407   b) 655   c) 252
2 N/A

Unit 8 Number problems
On track
1 a) 57; 43 + 57 = 100
  b) 73; 27 + 73 = 100
  c) 44; 56 + 44 = 100
  d) 68; 32 + 68 = 100
2 a) 114; 40 + 14 = 54
  b) 233; 60 +33 = 93
  c) 432; 50 + 32 = 82
  d) 351; 30 + 51 = 81
3 a) 29; 40 – 11 = 29
  b) 37; 60 – 23 = 37
  c) 43; 80 – 37 = 43
  d) 49; 100 – 51 = 49
Aiming higher
1 a) 79 marbles altogether.
  b) Jim has 5 more marbles than Ali.
  c) 42 + 37 = 79;
     42 – 37 = 5
2 50 – 17 = 33.
  Sam sold 33 pies.
Using and applying
1 N/A
2 N/A

Unit 9 Multiplication and division facts
On track
1 a) 12   b) 24
  c) 32   d) 32
  e) 18   f) 28
  g) 48   h) 72
  i) 21   j) 36
  k) 40   l) 56
2 All except i; multiples of even numbers are even.
Aiming higher
1 a) 8
  b) 7
  c) 9
  d) 4
2 a) 4 × 6 = 24;
     24 ÷ 4 = 6;
     24 ÷ 6 = 4
  b) 3 × 5 = 15;
     15 ÷ 3 = 5;
     15 ÷ 5 = 3
  c) 2 × 8 = 16;
     16 ÷ 2 = 8;
     16 ÷ 8 = 2
  d) 5 × 4 = 20;
     20 ÷ 5 = 4;
     20 ÷ 4 = 5
3 One, because the numbers are square numbers.
  a) 3 × 3 = 9; 9 ÷ 3 = 3
  b) 4 × 4 = 16; 16 ÷ 4 = 4
  c) 5 × 5 = 25; 25 ÷ 5 = 5
  d) 8 × 8 = 64; 64 ÷ 8 = 8

Using and applying
1 24
2 24, 36
3 48, 72
4 N/A

Unit 10   Multiplication and division
On track
1 a) 4×7; 28   b) 9×4; 36
   c) 7×6; 42   d) 7×8; 56
2 a) $32 \div 8$; 4   b) $48 \div 8$; 6
   c) $64 \div 8$; 8   d) $72 \div 8$; 9

Aiming higher
1 a) $81 \times 4 = 324$
   b) $62 \times 5 = 310$
   c) $63 \times 8 = 504$
   d) $64 \times 3 = 192$
   e) $34 \times 7 = 238$
   f) $85 \times 3 = 255$
   g) $42 \times 8 = 336$
   h) $57 \times 5 = 285$
2 a) $63 \div 3 = 21$
   b) $64 \div 4 = 16$
   c) $72 \div 3 = 24$
   d) $76 \div 4 = 19$
   e) $88 \div 4 = 22$
   f) $88 \div 8 = 11$
   g) $96 \div 4 = 24$
   h) $95 \div 5 = 19$

Using and applying
1 a) With 21 eggs, 3 rows of eggs can be filled.
   b) There will be 3 eggs in the partly filled row.
2 On Tuesday, 3 egg boxes will be needed for 18 eggs.
3 On Wednesday, 4 egg boxes will be needed for 19 eggs. An extra box for the spare egg over 18.

Unit 11   More number problems
On track
1 a) $17 + 5 = 22$. 'More than' indicates addition.
   b) $40 - 16 = 24$. 'Less than' indicates subtraction.
2 a) $17 \times 2 = 34$. 'Double' indicates 'multiply by 2'.
   b) $72 \div 2 = 36$. 'Half of' indicates 'divide by 2'.

Aiming higher
1 $? + 7 = 19$.
   My number is 12.
2 $? - 5 = 18$.
   My number is 23.
3 $? \times 2 + 3 = 19$.
   My number is 8.
4 N/A

Using and applying
1 13 cards.
2 2 eggs and 130g of butter, caster sugar and self-raising flour.
3 12 different outfits.

Unit 12   Finding fractions
On track
1 a) $\frac{1}{4}$ b) $\frac{1}{6}$ c) $\frac{1}{8}$
   d) $\frac{1}{10}$ e) $\frac{1}{12}$
2 a) $\frac{2}{12}$ b) $\frac{3}{12}$ c) $\frac{4}{12}$
   d) $\frac{6}{12}$ e) $\frac{9}{12}$

Aiming higher
1 a) $\frac{3}{12} = \frac{1}{4}$ b) $\frac{4}{12} = \frac{1}{3}$ c) $\frac{10}{12} = \frac{5}{6}$
2 a) $\frac{26}{52} = \frac{1}{2}$ b) $\frac{13}{52} = \frac{1}{4}$ c) $\frac{4}{52} = \frac{1}{13}$

Using and applying
1 a) 15 minutes is $\frac{1}{4}$ of an hour.
   b) 30 minutes is $\frac{1}{2}$ of an hour.
2 $\frac{5}{6} > \frac{3}{4}$

Unit 13   Comparing and ordering fractions
On track
1 $\frac{1}{3} + \frac{2}{3} = 1$
2 a) $\frac{1}{6} + \frac{5}{6} = 1$
   b) $\frac{2}{6} + \frac{4}{6} = 1$
   c) $\frac{3}{6} + \frac{3}{6} = 1$

Aiming higher
1 $\frac{1}{12}, \frac{1}{9}, \frac{1}{7}, \frac{1}{3}, \frac{1}{2}$
2 $\frac{8}{9}, \frac{7}{9}, \frac{5}{9}, \frac{2}{9}, \frac{1}{9}$
3 $\frac{1}{4}, \frac{1}{2}, \frac{7}{12}, \frac{3}{4}, \frac{5}{6}$
   Accept suitable shaded diagrams.

Using and applying
1 Any two fractions that add to $\frac{3}{4}$, e.g. $\frac{1}{4}$ and $\frac{1}{2}$
2 $x + 2x + 3x = 1$; $x = \frac{1}{6}$ and the three fractions are: $\frac{1}{6}, \frac{1}{3}, \frac{1}{2}$

Unit 14   Calculations with fractions
On track
1 a) $\frac{3}{5} + \frac{1}{5} = \frac{4}{5}$
   b) $\frac{3}{6} + \frac{1}{6} = \frac{4}{6}$ $(= \frac{2}{3})$
   c) $\frac{4}{7} + \frac{2}{7} = \frac{6}{7}$
   d) $\frac{5}{9} + \frac{2}{9} = \frac{7}{9}$
2 a) $\frac{4}{5} - \frac{1}{5} = \frac{3}{5}$
   b) $\frac{3}{6} - \frac{1}{6} = \frac{2}{6}$ $(= \frac{1}{3})$
   c) $\frac{4}{7} - \frac{2}{7} = \frac{2}{7}$
   d) $\frac{5}{9} - \frac{2}{9} = \frac{3}{9}$ $(= \frac{1}{3})$

Aiming higher
1 a) $\frac{1}{6}$
   b) $\frac{5}{6}$
   c) $\frac{2}{6}$ $(= \frac{1}{3})$
2 a) $\frac{3}{12}$ $(= \frac{1}{4})$
   b) $1 - \frac{1}{4} = \frac{3}{4}$
   c) $\frac{2}{12}$ $(= \frac{1}{6})$

Using and applying
1 $\frac{1}{4} + \frac{1}{2} = \frac{3}{4}$; $15 + 30 = 45$
2 N/A

Unit 15   Tenths
On track
1 $\frac{1}{10}, \frac{2}{10}, \frac{3}{10}, \frac{4}{10}, \frac{5}{10}, \frac{6}{10}, \frac{7}{10}, \frac{8}{10}, \frac{9}{10}$
2 $\frac{9}{10}, \frac{8}{10}, \frac{7}{10}, \frac{6}{10}, \frac{5}{10}, \frac{4}{10}, \frac{3}{10}, \frac{2}{10}, \frac{1}{10}$

3 a) $\frac{1}{10}$
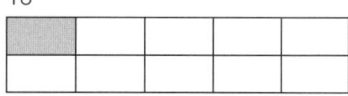
   b) $\frac{3}{10}$
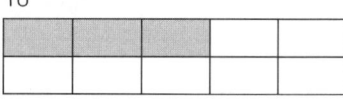
   c) $\frac{5}{10}$
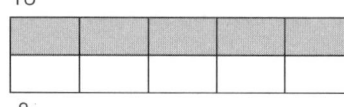
   d) $\frac{8}{10}$
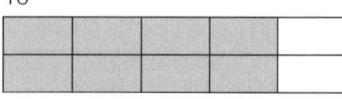

Aiming higher
1
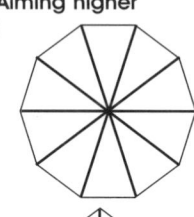
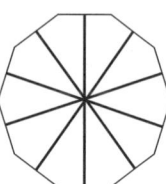
2
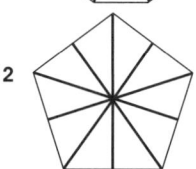

Using and applying
1 a) 4p
   b) 10p
2 50p

Unit 16   Units of measure
On track
1 1000
2 10
3 1000
4 1000

Aiming higher
1 a) 1000g   b) 100mm
   c) 100cm   d) 1000ml
   e) 69m   f) 100kg
2 a) 2000g   b) 200mm
   c) 500cm   d) 2000ml
   e) 65m   f) 100kg

Using and applying
1 3 packets of pudding rice
2 8 glasses

Unit 17   Perimeters
On track
1 a) 16cm   b) 18cm
   c) 16cm   d) 22cm
2 B: count the triangles along the sides.
3 a) $8 \times 35mm = 280mm$
   b) $3 \times 9cm = 27cm$

Aiming higher
1 $28cm \div 4 = 7cm$
2 $42m - 8m - 8m = 26m$
   Longest side = $26cm \div 2 = 13cm$

Using and applying
1 Shortest perimeter: 14 (3 by 4)
   Longest perimeter: 26 (1 by 12)
2 $8 \times 12cm = 96cm$

Unit 18 Calendars

On track

1)

Month	Days
January	31
February	28 or 29
March	31
April	30
May	31
June	30
July	31
August	31
September	30
October	31
November	30
December	31

2 365 unless it's a leap year; then 366.
3 2016 is a leap year, because 4 divides exactly into 2016. The next leap year is 2020.

Aiming higher
N/A

Using and applying
1 N/A
2 9 February 2016
3 20 February 2016

Unit 19 Clocks

On track
1 There are 60 seconds in one minute, 60 minutes in one hour, and 24 hours in one day.
2 a) 12:00 b) 00:00
   c) 18:20 d) 07:50
3 a) 9:30 a.m. b) 3:15 p.m.
   c) 7:50 a.m. d) 8:10 p.m.

Aiming higher
1 a) 5 b) 10
   c) 6 d) 9
2 a) 22:30 b) 13:15
   c) 16:45 d) 19:00

Using and applying
1 N/A

Unit 20 Intervals of time

On track
1 N/A
2 a) 11:45 a.m.
   b) 3:15 p.m.
3 8:20 a.m.

Aiming higher
1 17:55
2 7 hours and 8 mins

Using and applying
1 The 09:35 takes 59 mins.
2 Emma arrives at 07:49. Next train to Wakefield is at 09:40. Emma has to wait 1 hour and 51 mins.

Unit 21 Money

On track
1 a) £135 + £25 = £160
   b) £162 + £150 = £312
   c) £57 − £25 = £32
   d) £750 − £175 = £575
2 a) £3.50 + £2.50 = £6
   b) £6.25 + £1.50 = £7.75
   c) £5.75 − £2.50 = £3.25
   d) £7.50 − £1.75 = £5.75
3 a) £3.55 + £2.70 = £6.25
   b) £6.65 + £1.70 = £8.35
   c) £5.75 − £2.80 = £2.95
   d) £7.80 − £1.95 = £5.85

Aiming higher
1 £6.58
2 £9.32
3 £4.80
4 £1.62
5 10p
6 £3.45

Using and applying
1 £9
2 £10.40

Unit 22 Lines

On track
N/A

Aiming higher
N/A

Using and applying
1 The surface of the water remains horizontal.
2 The final position of the string is vertical.

Unit 23 Right angles

On track
1 c)

2 a) 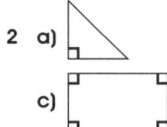 b)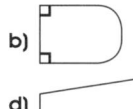

   c) 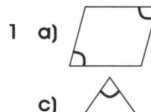 d)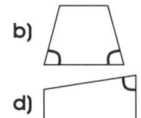

Aiming higher
1 a) 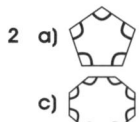 b)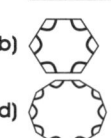

   c) d)

2 a) b)

   c) d)

Using and applying
1 The diagonals of a square intersect at right angles.
2 The diagonals of a rectangle intersect to create two angles less than a right angle (called acute angles) and two angles greater than a right angle (called obtuse angles).
3 N/A

Unit 24 Angles and turning

On track
1 Walk 1 pace; turn left through a quarter turn; walk 5 paces; turn left through a quarter turn; walk 1 pace; turn left through a quarter turn; walk 5 paces; turn left through a quarter turn
2 Walk 3 paces; turn left through a quarter turn; walk 3 paces; turn left through a quarter turn; walk 3 paces; turn left through a quarter turn; walk 3 paces; turn left through a quarter turn
(or all right turns).
3 Walk 5 paces; turn left through a quarter turn; walk 5 paces; turn left through a quarter turn; walk 5 paces; turn left through a quarter turn; walk 5 paces; turn left through a quarter turn
(or all right turns to match their answer to Q2).
4 Walk 7 paces; turn right through a quarter turn; walk 7 paces; turn right through a quarter turn; walk 7 paces; turn right through a quarter turn; walk 7 paces; turn right through a quarter turn
(or all left turns to match their answer to Q2).

Aiming higher
1 a) Starting top left, facing down:
      walk 2 paces;
      turn left through a quarter turn;
      walk 5 paces;
      turn left through a quarter turn;
      walk 1 pace;
      turn left through a quarter turn;
      walk 4 paces;
      turn right through a quarter turn;
      walk 1 pace;
      turn left through a quarter turn;
      walk 1 pace;
      turn left through a quarter turn.
   b) Starting top left, facing down:
      walk 1 pace;
      turn right through a quarter turn;
      walk 2 paces;
      turn left through a quarter turn;
      walk 1 pace;
      turn left through a quarter turn;
      walk 2 paces;
      turn right through a quarter turn;
      walk 1 pace;
      turn left through a quarter turn;
      walk 1 pace;
      turn left through a quarter turn;
      walk 1 pace;
      turn right through a quarter turn;
      walk 2 paces; turn left through a quarter turn;
      walk 1 pace;
      turn left through a quarter turn;
      walk 2 paces;
      turn right through a quarter turn;
      walk 1 pace;
      turn left through a quarter turn;
      walk 1 pace;
      turn left through a quarter turn.
2 N/A
3 N/A

Using and applying
N/A

Unit 25 2-D and 3-D shapes

On track
1 a) rectangle
   b) right-angled triangle
   c) circle
   d) isosceles triangle
   e) hexagon
   f) square
   g) pentagon
   h) trapezium
   i) kite
   j) rhombus/diamond
   k) oval/ellipse
2 N/A
3 a) sphere
   b) cube
   c) cuboid
   d) cone
   e) triangular prism
   f) cylinder
   g) hexagonal prism
   h) pentagonal prism

Aiming higher
1 Rectangle
2 Cube; square
3 a) Square-based pyramid
   b) Cube, cuboid

Using and applying
1 Regular = all sides the same length
2 N/A

Unit 26   Pictograms

On track

1 **a)** 8 children
  b) 6 children
  c) 18 children
2 **a)** 20 trees
  b) 26 trees

Aiming higher

1 **a)** 5 children
  b) 6 children
  c) 1 children

Using and applying

N/A

Unit 27   Bar charts

On track

1 **a)** 5 patients
  b) 4 patients

Aiming higher

1 **a)** 3 matches
  b) 5 matches

Using and applying

N/A

Unit 28 Solving data problems

On track

1 **a)** e.g. How many bring sandwiches?
     How many eat a school meal? Which
     was the most popular option? Which
     was the least popular option? How
     many more children had sandwiches
     than went home for lunch?
  b) N/A
2 **a)** e.g. How many prefer roast potatoes?
     How many prefer mashed potatoes?
     How many prefer jacket potatoes?
     Which was the most popular option?
     Which was the least popular option?
  b) N/A

Aiming higher

1 **a)** 'What is your first name?'
  b) N/A
2 **a)** Gender (B/G)
  b) N/A

Using and applying

N/A

Unit 29 More problem solving

On track

1 **a)** $214 \div 4$
2 **d)** 8×4

Aiming higher

N/A

Using and applying

1 **a)** £10 − £4.29
  b) Jill should get £5.71 in change.
2 $2 \times 78p + £1.20 / 2 = £1.56 + 60p =$
   £2.16. Jemima spends £2.16 altogether.

On Track

1 Do these calculations.

a) $\frac{3}{5} + \frac{1}{5}$ **b)** $\frac{3}{6} + \frac{1}{6}$ **c)** $\frac{4}{7} + \frac{2}{7}$ **d)** $\frac{5}{9} + \frac{2}{9}$

Show how you worked out each answer, using a diagram.

2 Do these calculations.

a) $\frac{4}{5} - \frac{1}{5}$ **b)** $\frac{3}{6} - \frac{1}{6}$ **c)** $\frac{4}{7} - \frac{2}{7}$ **d)** $\frac{5}{9} - \frac{2}{9}$

Show how you worked out each answer, using a diagram.

Aiming Higher

1 This cake is marked into six portions.

a) If Amy eats one portion, what fraction of the cake has she eaten?

b) What fraction of the cake is left?

c) If Ali eats two portions, what fraction of the cake has he eaten?

2 A bar of chocolate with 12 squares is shared between friends.

a) Ali, Jamil and Paulo eat one square each. What fraction of the bar has been eaten?

b) What fraction of the bar is left?

c) Jamil eats one more square. What fraction of the bar has he eaten altogether?

Using and Applying

1 It takes a quarter of an hour to walk to the bus stop and the bus trip takes half an hour. How long does the journey take altogether? Give your answer as a fraction of an hour, and then in minutes.

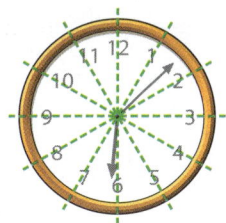

2 Make up a fraction problem of your own and share it with a friend. Compare your answers.

15 Tenths

What do you need to know?

- How to count in halves and quarters to ten

What will you learn?

- To recognise how tenths arise
- How to count up and down in tenths

Example

The shape is divided into ten equal parts. Each square is $\frac{1}{10}$ of the whole shape.

$\frac{1}{10}$	$\frac{1}{10}$	$\frac{1}{10}$	$\frac{1}{10}$	$\frac{1}{10}$
$\frac{1}{10}$	$\frac{1}{10}$	$\frac{1}{10}$	$\frac{1}{10}$	$\frac{1}{10}$

1 of the 10 squares is shaded.

One tenth of the whole shape is shaded.

These two pizzas are each divided into five parts so that each of ten people can have an equal share.

$2 \div 10 = \frac{2}{10} = \frac{1}{5}$

Key facts

The unit fraction $\frac{1}{10}$ is called a **tenth**. It is ten times smaller than the number 1.

Language

The word **tenth** is used in other ways too:
- A **tenth share** is what you get if you divided something, like a pizza or a cake, into ten equal parts.
- Counting in order from 1 to 10, ten is the **tenth number**. First, second, third, fourth, fifth, sixth, seventh, eighth, ninth, tenth.

A **decagon** is a ten-sided shape. A **pentagon** is a five-sided shape.

On Track

1 Fill in the gaps in this sequence.

$\frac{1}{10}$ ... $\frac{3}{10}$ ... ... $\frac{6}{10}$ ... ... $\frac{9}{10}$

2 Fill in the gaps in this sequence.

... $\frac{8}{10}$ ... ... $\frac{5}{10}$ ... ... $\frac{2}{10}$ ...

3 Copy this shape four times and then shade these fractions of the shape.

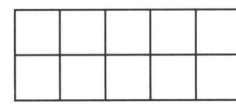

a) $\frac{1}{10}$ **b)** $\frac{3}{10}$ **c)** $\frac{5}{10}$ **d)** $\frac{8}{10}$

Aiming Higher

1 This decagon has ten equal sides.
Copy this shape and draw lines on it to divide it into tenths.
Compare your drawing with your friend's.
Did you divide the decagon in the same way?

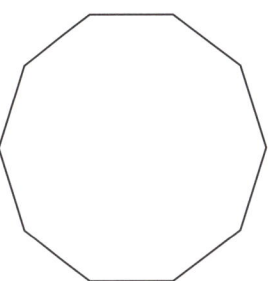

2 This pentagon has five equal sides.
Copy this shape and draw lines on it to divide it into tenths.
Compare your drawing with your friend's.
Did you divide the pentagon in the same way?

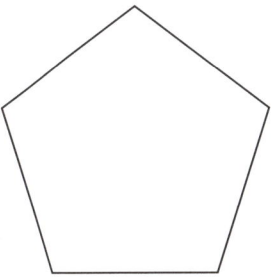

Using and Applying

1 A one-pence coin (1p) is worth one tenth of a ten-pence coin (10p).

a) What is one-tenth of 40p?

b) What is one-tenth of £1?

2 A taxi ride costs £5 and Harry decides to give a tip of one-tenth to the driver. How much tip will Harry give?

16 Units of measure

What do you need to know?

- How to choose appropriate standard units to measure length/height, mass and capacity
- How to compare and order lengths, mass, capacity and volume, and record the results using $<$, $>$ and $=$
- How to read relevant scales to the nearest numbered unit

What will you learn?

- How to measure, compare, add and subtract lengths, mass, volume and capacity

Example

Last year Keith's best high jump was 1 metre 75 centimetres. This year his best jump is 2 metres 10 centimetres. By how much has Keith improved?

To find the difference between two heights, you need subtraction.

$$2m\ 10cm = 210cm \quad 1m\ 75cm = 175cm$$

$$210cm - 175cm = 35cm$$

Keith improved his performance by 35 centimetres.

Key facts

Length and height are measured in metres (m), centimetres (cm) and millimetres (mm).
Mass is measured in kilograms (kg) and grams (g).
Volume and capacity are measured in litres (l) and millilitres (ml).

Language

Centi- means one-hundredth part. $1m = 100cm$
Milli- means one-thousandth part. 1 litre $= 1000ml$
Kilo- means one thousand times. $1kg = 1000g$

On Track

1. How many times bigger than a gram is a kilogram?
2. How many times smaller than a centimetre is a millimetre?
3. How many times bigger than a millilitre is a litre?
4. How many times smaller than a metre is a millimetre?

Aiming Higher

1. Do these sums. Give your answer in the same units as the question.
   a) 750g + 250g
   b) 35mm + 65mm
   c) 45cm + 55cm
   d) 150ml + 850ml
   e) 17m + 52m
   f) 85kg + 15kg

2. Do these sums. Give your answer in the same units as the question.
   a) 2750g − 750g
   b) 285mm − 85mm
   c) 545cm − 45cm
   d) 2850ml − 850ml
   e) 82m − 17m
   f) 350kg − 250kg

Using and Applying

1. A packet of pudding rice contains 475g.
   You need 1kg of rice for a recipe.
   How many packets will you have to open?

2. How many glasses holding 150ml can be filled from this jug of orange juice?

17 Perimeters

What do you need to know?

- How to carry out simple additions
- How to carry out simple multiplications and divisions

What will you learn?

- How to measure the perimeter of simple 2-D shapes

Example

A square lawn has sides 15 paces long.

If you walk around the edge of the lawn,
how many paces would you walk?

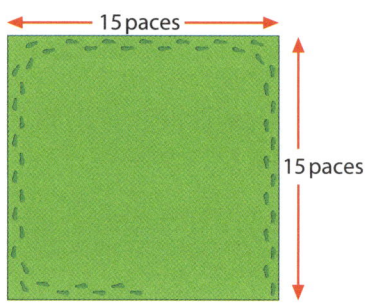

Each side is 15 paces long.
There are 4 sides.

$15 + 15 + 15 + 15 = 60$, or $4 \times 15 = 60$

You would walk 60 paces.

Key facts

To calculate the perimeter of a 2-D shape, add up the lengths of all of the sides.

Language

Perimeter: the total distance along the sides of a shape
A 2-D shape with sides all the same length is called **regular**; otherwise, it is **irregular**. A regular triangle is **equilateral**. A regular rectangle is a **square**.
Pentagon: a five-sided shape   **Hexagon**: a six-sided shape
Heptagon: a seven-sided shape   **Octagon**: an eight-sided shape

On Track

1 Copy these four shapes onto centimetre squared paper.

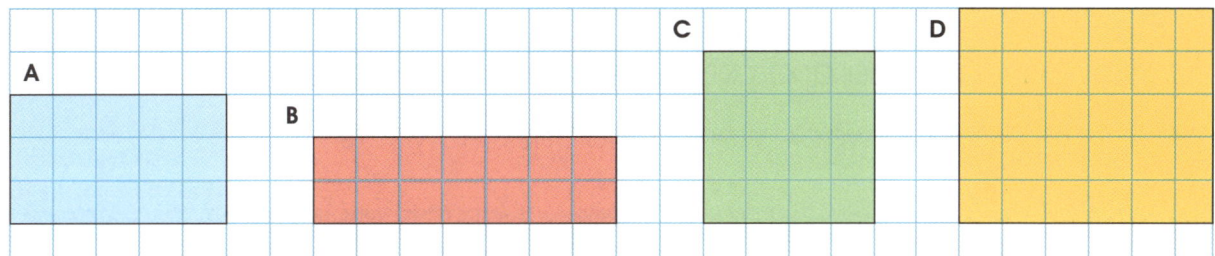

What is the perimeter of each shape?

2 Which of these two shapes has the longer perimeter?
Explain how you worked this out.

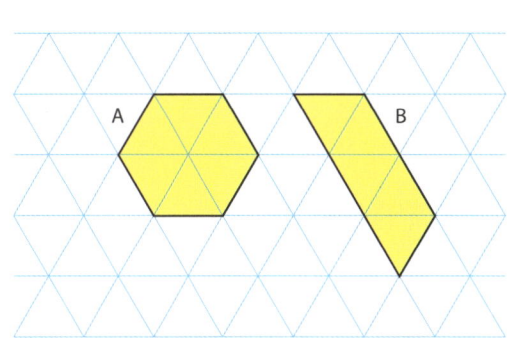

3 What is the perimeter of these shapes?
   a) A regular octagon with sides of 35 mm
   b) An equilateral triangle with sides of 9 cm

Aiming Higher

1 The perimeter of a square is 28 cm.
What is the length of one side?

?cm

2 A rectangle had a perimeter of 42 m.
The shortest side is 8 m long.
   a) What is the length of the longest side?
   b) How did you work it out?

8 m

?m

Using and Applying

1 On centimetre-squared paper, draw different rectangles, each using exactly 12 squares. Which shape has the shortest perimeter? Which has the longest perimeter?

2 Keisha wants to wrap this present with ribbon.
The present is 12 centimetres long and 12 centimetres wide.
   a) How long a piece of ribbon will Keisha need?
   b) How did you work this out?

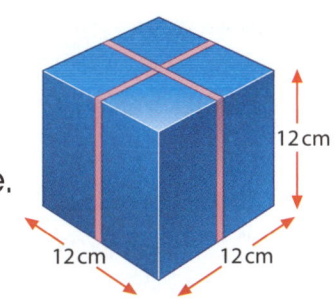

12 cm

12 cm   12 cm

18 Calendars

What do you need to know?

- How to recognise and use the language of dates
- The days of the week, weeks, months and years

What will you learn?

- The number of days in each month, year and leap year

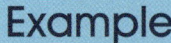 **Example**

This rhyme might help you to remember how many days there are in each month.

30 days has September,
April, June and November.
All the rest have 31
excepting February alone,
which has 28 days,
29 in a leap year.

Key facts

There are 365 days in a common year, but 366 days in a leap year. 2000 was a leap year. 2100, 2200 and 2300 will not be leap years, but 2400 will be.

Language

Leap year: happens every fourth year, when the year is exactly divisible by 4, except for years ending with '00' when they must be exactly divisible by 400.

Common year: a year that is not a leap year.

 **On Track**

1 Write down today's date and then complete this table for this year.

Month	Number of days	Month	Number of days
January		July	
February		August	
March		September	
April		October	
May		November	
June		December	

2 Use your table to calculate the total number of days this year.

3 Is this year a leap year? Explain how you know.
When is the next leap year?

 **Aiming Higher**

1 How many days are there in the month of your birthday?

2 How many days is it to the end of this month?

3 How many days is it to the end of next month?

 **Using and Applying**

1 What day of the week is Christmas Day this year?

2 Pancake Day falls on the second Tuesday of February in 2016.
What date will this be?

3 Kathy's birthday in 2016 is on 17 February. She has a party on the
Saturday after her birthday. What is the date of Kathy's party?

19 Clocks

What do you need to know?

- How to tell and write the time to 5 minutes including quarter past/to the hour
- How to draw hands on a clock face to show these times

What will you learn?

- How to tell and write the time from an analogue clock, including using Roman numerals from I to XII
- How to tell and write the time from 12-hour and 24-hour digital clocks

Example

A 24-hour clock shows times from 00:00 to 23:59.

12 noon is in the middle of the day.

12 midnight is in the middle of the night.

Key facts

24 hours = 1 day   60 minutes = 1 hour   60 seconds = 1 minute

Analogue clocks and 12-hour digital clocks show the time in hours and minutes, but not the time of day as in morning or afternoon.

Roman numerals 1 to 12 are: I, II, III, IV, V, VI, VII, VIII, IX, X, XI, XII

Language

Analogue clock: uses hands on a clockface dial, rotating to show the time passing

Digital clock: uses digits (not a dial and hands) to show the time, but only to the nearest minute (or nearest second for a stopwatch)

a.m. stands for *ante meridiem* – before midday

p.m. stands for *post meridiem* – after midday

 **On Track**

1 Complete this statement: There are … seconds in one minute, … minutes in one hour, and … hours in one day.

2 How would these times be shown on a 24-hour digital clock?
  a) Twelve noon
  b) Twelve midnight
  c) Twenty minute past six in the evening
  d) Ten minutes to eight in the morning

3 Write these times using a.m. or p.m.
  a)
  b)
  c)
  d)

 **Aiming Higher**

1 What are the values of these Roman numerals?
  a) V   **b)** X   **c)** VI   **d)** IX

2 Write these post meridiem times in this form: 12:15.
  a)
  b)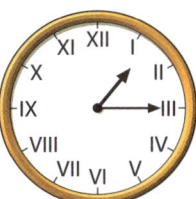
  c)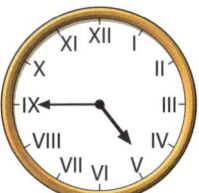
  d)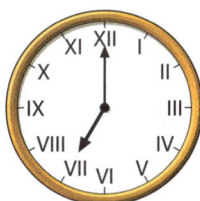

 **Using and Applying**

1 **a)** What is the time on the clock on the wall, to the nearest five minutes? Write your answer using a.m. or p.m.
  b) What time will it be in 12 hours' time?
  c) What time will it be in 24 hours' time?

2 **a)** What is the exact time on the clock on the wall, to the nearest minute? Write your answer using a.m. or p.m.
  b) What time will it be in 12 hours' time?
  c) What time will it be in 24 hours' time?

20 Intervals of time

What do you need to know?

- How to tell and write the time to the nearest 5 minutes
- How to tell and write the time from digital clocks

What will you learn?

- How to estimate and read time to the nearest minute
- How to compare durations of events, for example to calculate the time taken up by particular events or tasks

Example

Thursday's maths lesson starts at 2:30 p.m. and ends at 3:15 p.m.

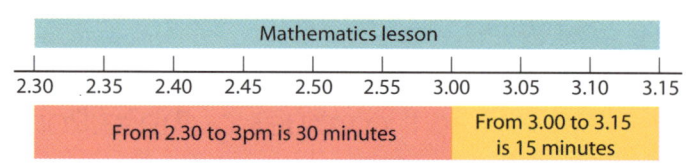

What is the length of the lesson?

$30 + 15 = 45$

The length of the lesson is 45 minutes.

A train leaves Nutfield at 8:40 a.m. and arrives at Gratton at 11:10 a.m.

How long is the train journey?

From 8:40 a.m. to 9 a.m. is 20 minutes.

From 9 a.m. to 11 a.m. is 2 hours.

From 11 a.m. to 11:10 a.m. is 10 minutes.

20 minutes + 2 hours + 10 minutes = 2 hours 30 minutes

The train journey takes 2 hours 30 minutes.

Key facts

There are 60 seconds in 1 minute. There are 60 minutes in 1 hour.

Language

a.m. is short for *ante meridiem* (before midday)

p.m. is short for *post meridiem* (after midday)

 **On Track**

1   What time is it on the clock on the wall, to the nearest minute?
    a) How long is it since the lesson started?
    b) How long is it until the lesson ends?

2   The time is 2:45 p.m.
    a) What time was it three hours ago?
    b) What time will it be in 30 minutes' time?

3   It takes 35 minutes to walk from home to school. Ben needs to be there by 8:55 a.m. By what time should Ben leave home?

 **Aiming Higher**

1   The time of Simon's digital watch is 18:02. His watch is seven minutes fast. What is the correct time?

2   A plane takes off on Wednesday at 22:57. It lands on Thursday at 06:05. How long is the flight in hours and minutes? Show how you calculated your answer.

 **Using and Applying**

Here is part of a timetable.

Newcastle	07:44	08:24	09:35	09:40	10:26
York	08:44	09:27	10:34	10:44	11:27
Leeds	09:10			11:10	
Wakefield	09:23			11:23	
Sheffield	09:53	10:23	11:23	11:53	12:23
Derby	10:24	10:57	11:57	12:24	12:57

1   Which train travels from Newcastle to York in the shortest time? And how long does it take?

2   Emma arrives at Newcastle five minutes after the 07:44 train has left. She wants to go to Wakefield. How much longer does she have to wait for the next train to Wakefield?

21 Money

What do you need to know?

● How to combine coins and notes of different values to make a particular value

What will you learn?

● How to add and subtract amounts of money to give change

Example

You can add and subtract amounts of money in the same way that you can add and subtract whole numbers.

£127		£300	£12.55		£10.00
+ £228	If there are no pence, just include a £ sign.	− £275	+ £7.50	If there are pence, they are written after the decimal point.	− £4.75
£355		£25	£20.05		£5.25

To give change, you can 'count on'. £4.75 + 25p = £5. £5 + £5 = £10.
Change to be given is 25p + £5 = £5.25

Key facts

£ stands for pounds. p stands for pence.
Ten 1p coins are equivalent to one 10p coin.

 =

Ten 10p coins are equivalent to one £1 coin.

 =

Language

When asked for the **total**, add the amounts together.
To work out **how much you have left**, subtract the amount of money you spent from how much you started with.

On Track

1 Do these calculations. Lay out your work carefully.
   a) £135 + £25   b) £162 + £150
   c) £57 − £25   d) £750 − £175

2 Do these calculations. Lay out your work carefully.
   a) £3.50 + £2.50   b) £6.25 + £1.50
   c) £5.75 − £2.50   d) £7.50 − £1.75

3 Do these calculations. Lay out your work carefully.
   a) £3.55 + £2.70   b) £6.65 + £1.70
   c) £5.75 − £2.80   d) £7.80 − £1.95

Aiming Higher

1 What is the total of £4.31 and £2.27?

2 Sanjay has saved £4.45. His sister Amber has saved £4.87. How much have they saved altogether?

3 James has £6.53 to spend. He spends £1.73. How much does he have left?

4 Dan goes shopping for his mum. The total cost is £3.38. He pays with a £5 note. How much change should he get?

5 I buy two comics that costs 45p each. How much change will I get from £1?

6 Amy wants to buy a toy costing £5.85. She has £2.40 saved. How much more does she need to buy the toy?

Using and Applying

1 Maria and her sister want to buy a coat that costs £60 as a present for their mother. Maria has £17. Her sister has double that amount. How much more money do they need?

2 Paul has £20. After buying toys costing £6.75 and £2.85, how much money does he have left?

22 Lines

What do you need to know?

- The mathematical vocabulary to describe position, direction and movement

What will you learn?

- How to identify horizontal and vertical lines
- How to identify perpendicular and parallel lines

Example

If you look around you there are horizontal and vertical lines everywhere.

There are also lots of parallel lines.

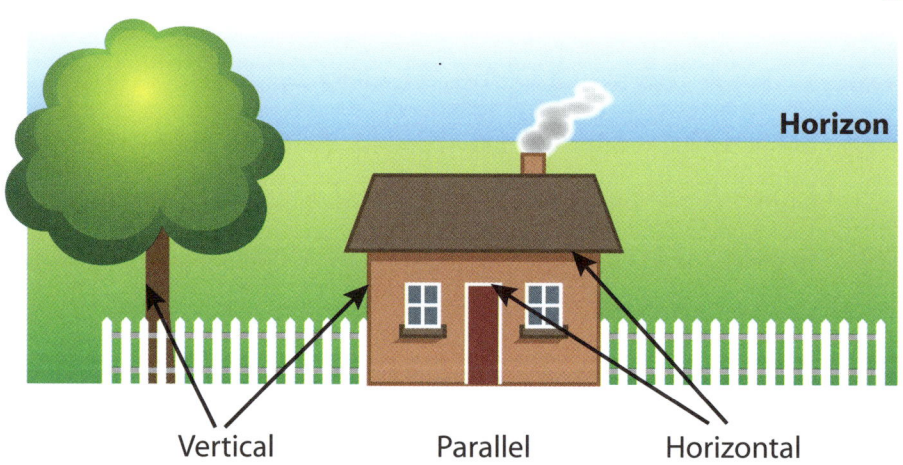

Vertical   Parallel   Horizontal

Key facts

A line is either straight or not straight; straight lines can be drawn with a ruler.
Two lines that never meet are parallel.
Two lines that do cross might intersect at right angles.
Then they are called perpendicular.

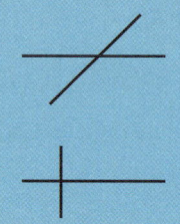

Language

A **horizontal** line follows the horizon.
A **vertical** line is at right angles to the horizontal.
Lines are **perpendicular** if they intersect at right angles.
Lines that remain the same distance from each other are called **parallel** lines. All horizontal lines are parallel to each other. All vertical lines are parallel to each other.

On Track

1. Look around you and identify four examples of lines that are not straight.
   Draw these lines and label them.

2. Look around you and identify four examples of straight lines.
   Draw these lines and label them.

3. Compare what you found for questions 1 and 2 with your friends.

Aiming Higher

1. Look around you and identify four examples of horizontal lines.
   Draw these lines and label them.

2. Look around you and identify four examples of vertical lines.
   Draw these lines and label them.

3. Look around you and identify four examples of pairs of parallel lines.
   Draw these lines and label them.

4. Look around you and identify four examples of pairs of perpendicular lines. Draw these lines and label them.

5. Compare what you found for questions 1 to 4 with your friends.

Using and Applying

1. Half fill a glass with water.
   Change the position of the glass so that the glass is tilted, first one way and then the other.
   Describe what happens to the surface of the water.

2. Attach an object to a piece of string and hold it up.

   Pull the object to one side and let it swing.
   Wait until it stops moving.
   Describe the final position of the string.

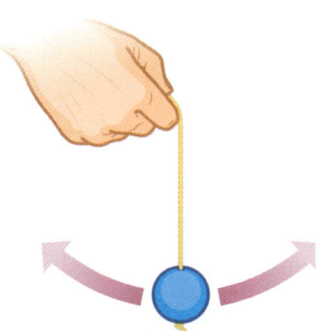

23 Right angles

What do you need to know?

- About quarter, half and three-quarter turns, clockwise and anticlockwise

What will you learn?

- How to identify right angles and whether angles are greater or less than a right angle
- That two right angles make a half turn, three make a three-quarter turn and four right angles make a complete turn

Example

When a horizontal line intersects a vertical line, they cross at right angles and create four right angles.

If one of the lines is off the horizontal or off the vertical, then angles smaller and bigger than a right angle are created.

Tip: Use the corner of a square piece of paper to check whether the angle is a right angle.

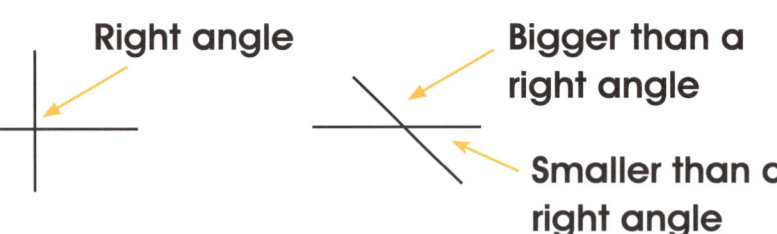

Right angle

Bigger than a right angle

Smaller than a right angle

Key facts

A right angle is a quarter turn.
Two right angles make a half turn.
Three right angles make a three-quarter turn.
Four right angles make a complete turn.

Language

Lines are **perpendicular** if they intersect at right angles.
Diagonal: a line drawn across a shape from one vertex (corner) to another vertex.

On Track

1 Right angles need not be between vertical and horizontal lines. Which of these pairs of lines intersect at right angles?

a)  b)  c)  d)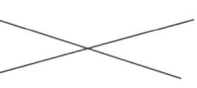

2 Right angles can also be seen at the corners of shapes. Mark all the right angles in these shapes.

a) 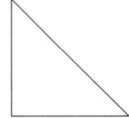 b)  c)  d)

Aiming Higher

1 In these shapes, mark any angles that are smaller than right angles.

a)  b)  c) 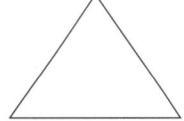 d)

2 In these shapes, mark any angles that are bigger than right angles.

a) 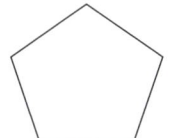 b) 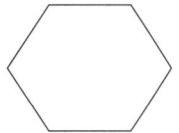 c) 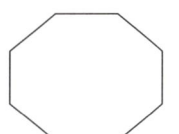 d)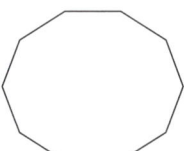

Using and Applying

1 Draw a square and then draw its diagonals.
Describe how the diagonals intersect.
What type of angle do they make?

2 Draw a rectangle and then draw its diagonals.
Describe how the diagonals intersect.
What types of angle do they make?

3 Experiment with diagonals of other shapes, and see what types of angle are made when they intersect.

24 Angles and turning

What do you need to know?

- Mathematical vocabulary to describe position, direction and movement

What will you learn?

- How to recognise angles as a property of shape
- How to associate angle as an amount of turning

Example

A shape can be described by a journey along the sides. Starting at the top left corner facing along the long side:

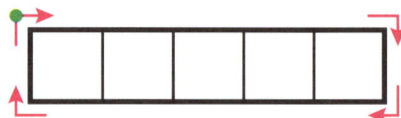

> Walk 5 paces, turn right through a quarter turn.
> Walk 1 pace, turn right through a quarter turn.
> Walk 5 paces, turn right through a quarter turn.
> Walk 1 pace, turn right through a quarter turn.

Notice that, to get back to the starting point and facing in the same direction, you will have made 4 quarter turns.

Key facts

Rotation is a movement which involves turning.
The amount of turning can be measured in **right angles**.
A right angle is a **quarter turn**.
Two right angles make a **half turn**.
Four right angles make a **complete turn**.

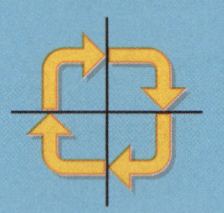

Language

Clockwise: the same direction as the hands on a clock

Anticlockwise: the opposite direction

On Track

1 Write the instructions to make another journey around this shape, this time in an anti-clockwise direction.

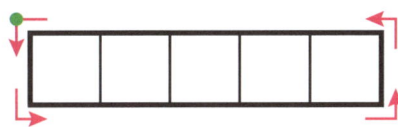

2 Write the instructions to make a journey around the sides of a square with side length of 3 paces.

3 Rewrite the instructions you wrote for question 2, to make a journey for a square with side length of 5 paces.

4 Rewrite the instructions you wrote for question 2, to make a journey for a square with side length of 7 paces, going in the opposite direction.

Aiming Higher

1 Write the instructions to make a journey around these shapes.

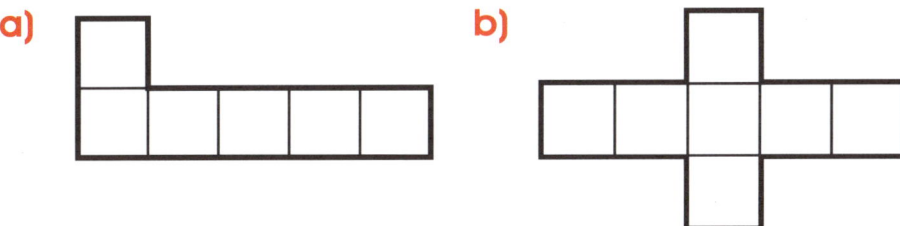

a)   b)

2 Rewrite the instructions you wrote for question 1, starting at a different point.

3 Rewrite the instructions you wrote for question 1, starting at a different point and going in the opposite direction.

Using and Applying

1 Write instructions for the route from your desk in the classroom to the classroom door, in paces and giving any turns you need to make. Then write the route for the return journey. Ask a friend to test out your instructions. Did they work?

2 Choose two rooms in your house, such as your bedroom and the kitchen. Give directions to go from one to the other. Test out your instructions. Did they work? Or would you have bumped into a wall?

25 2-D and 3-D shapes

What do you need to know?

- Properties of 2-D shapes: number of sides and symmetry
- Properties of 3-D shapes: number of edges, vertices and faces

What will you learn?

- How to draw 2-D and make 3-D shapes
- How to recognise 3-D shapes in different orientations

Example

To draw a 2-D shape, first check how many sides it has. Note any special properties, such as right angles, equal sides or parallel lines.

Draw shapes with right angles on squared paper.

Draw equilateral triangles and hexagons on an isometric grid.

Key facts

A **polygon** is a 2-D shape made only from straight lines.

hexagon

A **non-polygon** includes lines that are not straight.

semicircle

A **polyhedron** is a 3-D solid with flat faces.

polyhedron

Language

A **regular** shape is one with all side lengths equal. A triangle may be regular (an **equilateral** triangle) or, if only two sides are equal, it is an **isosceles** triangle. If all sides are different, the triangle is **scalene**.
An **acute** angle is less than a right angle. An **obtuse** angle is greater than a right angle, but less than two right angles.

On Track

1   Write one or more names for each shape.

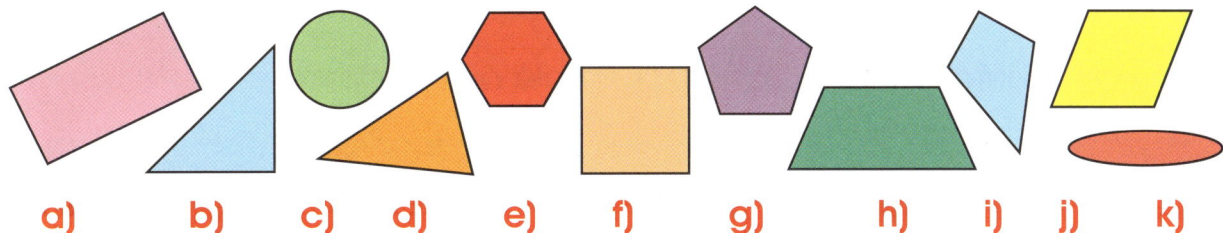

a)   b)   c)   d)   e)   f)   g)   h)   i)   j)   k)

2   Use isometric paper to draw and label these shapes.
   a) An equilateral triangle   b) An isosceles triangle
   c) A diamond   d) A regular hexagon

3   Give the full name for each of these solids.

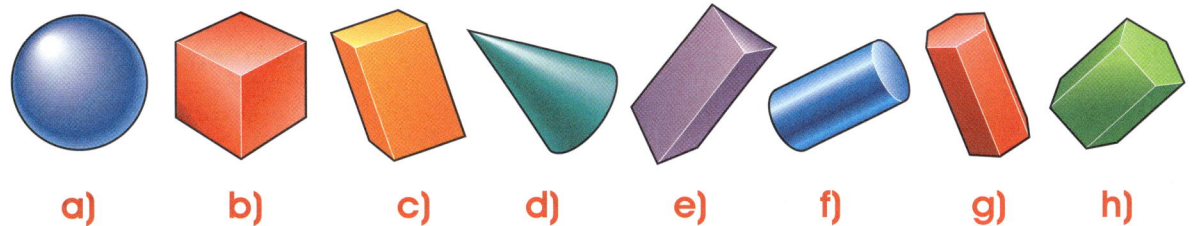

a)   b)   c)   d)   e)   f)   g)   h)

Aiming Higher

1   A 2-D shape has four right angles. It has four sides that are not all the same length. What is the name of the shape?

2   What 3-D shape has the same 2-D shape for all its faces?
   What is the 2-D shape? Make this shape.

3   a) I am thinking of a 3-D solid. It has a square base. Its four other faces are triangles. What is the name of this solid?
   b) Name two other 3-D shapes that have at least one square face.

Using and Applying

1   What is the difference between a regular and an irregular polygon? Draw two polygons to explain your answer.

2   Look at containers in your kitchen cupboard.
   What shapes are used to hold soup, cereals or other foods? Sketch some examples and compare yours with your friends.

26 Pictograms

What do you need to know?

- How to interpret and construct simple pictograms

What will you learn?

- How to answer questions such as 'How many more?' and 'How many fewer?' using information presented in pictograms

Example

There are 24 children in Class B.

This pictogram shows how they came to school today.

Notice the scale:
☺ represents 2 children.
A halved symbol indicates half of the scale amount.
☾ represents 1 child.

Ways of coming to school today	
	Number of children
Car	☺ ☺
Bus	☺ ☺ ☺ ☺ ☺ ☾
Walk	☺
Bicycle	☺ ☺ ☾

☺ represents 2 children

The number of children who cycle to school is ☺ ☺ ☾ = 2 + 2 + 1 = 5

Key facts

The total number of symbols in a pictogram, together with the scale, tells you the total number in the survey.

Language

Survey: an investigation to find out something, e.g. the type of traffic that passes the school gate, the shoe sizes worn in Year 3
Pictogram: diagram that shows the frequency of an event, e.g. the number of children who wear size 2 shoes
Frequency: the number of times something happens, e.g. how many times a six is rolled on a dice
Scale: amount that each symbol on a pictogram is worth

On Track

1 This pictogram shows the favourite ways of coming to school of the 24 children in Class B.

a) How many children prefer to come to school by car?

b) How many children prefer to come to school by bus?

c) How many prefer not to walk?

Favourite ways of coming to school	
	Number of children
Car	☺ ☺ ☺ ☺
Bus	☺ ☺ ☺
Walk	☺ ☺ ☺
Bicycle	☺ ☺

 ☺ represents 2 children

2 Some children measured the heights of trees in a wood. Here are their results.

a) How many trees were up to 10 m tall?

b) How many trees were between 10 m and 20 m tall?

Height	Number of trees
Up to 10 m	🌳 🌳 🌳 🌳 🌳
Between 10 m and 20 m	🌳 🌳 🌳 🌳 🌳 🌳 🌳

🌳 represents 4 trees

Aiming Higher

1 Look back at the pictogram on the previous page, which shows how the 24 children in Class B came to school today.

a) How many children cycled to school today?

b) How many more children came by bus?

c) How many fewer came by car?

Using and Applying

1 Choose a topic and present your own data in a pictogram.

2 Working in groups of 2 or 3, interpret the pictograms produced by others in your group. What does their pictogram tell you? Ask questions involving 'more' and 'fewer'.

27 Bar charts

What do you need to know?

- How to interpret and construct tally charts and block diagrams

What will you learn?

- How to answer questions such as 'How many more?' and 'How many fewer?' using information presented in scaled bar charts

Example

This bar chart shows the results of a survey of vehicles that passed the school gate between 2.30 p.m. and 3.30 p.m.

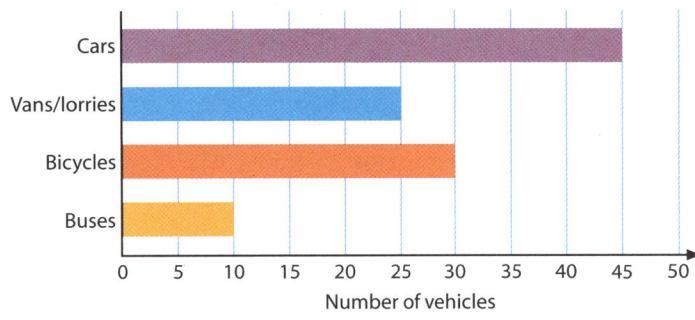

Notice that, while the frequency is a continuous scale, the bars are kept separate as there is no 'ordering' of the vehicles.
They are all different from each other.

From this bar chart, we can see that there were 25 vans, 10 buses and 30 bicycles. So we answer questions like:

How many **more** bicycles were there than buses? Answer: 20

How many **fewer** vans were there than bicycles? Answer: 5

Key facts

On a bar chart, you must use equal intervals along each scale.

Language

Frequency: the number of times something happens, like throwing a six on a dice

On Track

1 A dentist made a survey of the number of fillings his patients had, and presented the results in a bar chart.

a) How many more patients had no fillings than had 4 fillings?

b) How many fewer patients had 3 or more fillings than had 1 filling?

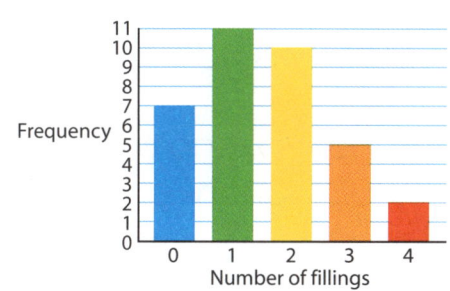

Aiming Higher

1 This bar chart shows the total number of goals scored in each first-round match of the World Cup in Germany in 2006.

a) In how many more matches were no goals scored, than 5 goals?

b) In how many fewer matches were three goals scored, than two goals?

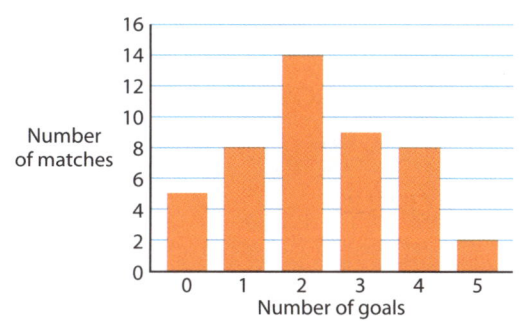

Using and Applying

1 Amy has invented a dice game. It involves throwing two normal dice. A person's score is the higher of the two numbers.

The score here is 5.

The score here is 3.

This bar chart shows the scores Amy found after some throws.

a) Ask yourself some questions using 'more' and 'fewer'.

b) Try your questions out on a friend.

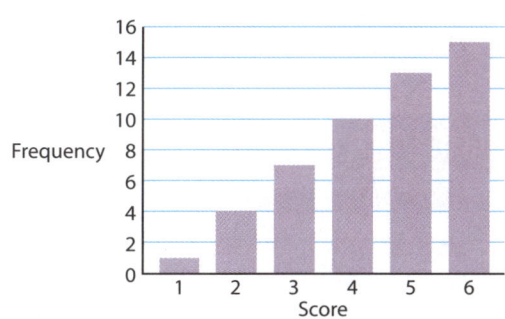

28 Solving data problems

What do you need to know?

- How to read and interpret data presented in table form or as pictograms and bar charts with scales

What will you learn?

- How to solve problems using information presented in pictograms, bar charts and tables

Example

This table shows the lunch choices of one year group.

Lunch choice	Frequency
School meal	35
Bring sandwiches	45
Go home	25

Here is a pictogram and a vertical bar chart showing the same data.

Lunch choice	Frequency
School meal	☺☺☺☺☺☺☺
Bring sandwiches	☺☺☺☺☺☺☺☺☺
Go home	☺☺☺☺☺
☺ = 5 pupils	

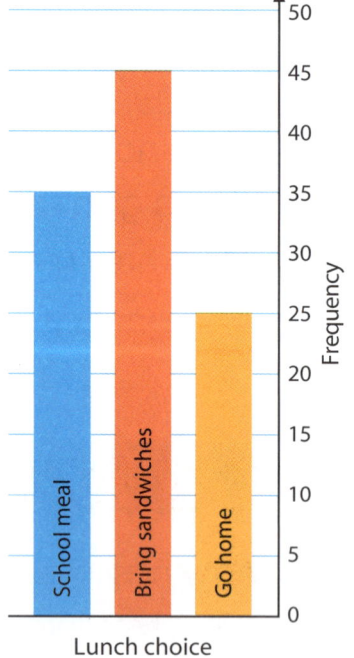

Some questions, like 'Which was the most popular choice?', can be answered just by looking at a chart.

Key facts

Data can be presented in a table, or as a chart.
A chart is a more visual method of presenting data.

Language

Pictogram: a chart using symbols to represent frequency
Bar chart: a chart using bars (either vertical or horizontal) to represent frequency

On Track

1 One question that can be answered by looking at the survey results on the opposite page is 'How many go home to lunch?'

   a) Write two more questions you can answer from the data.

   b) Swap questions with a friend and answer their questions.

2 This pictogram shows how the children who stay for school lunches like their potatoes cooked. One question that can be answered from this data is 'How many children prefer chips?'

   a) Write two more questions you can answer from the data.

   b) Swap questions with a friend and answer their questions.

Potatoes	Frequency
Roast	☺
Mashed	☺
Chips	☺ ☺
Jacket	☺ ☺ ☺

☺ = 5 pupils

Aiming Higher

1 You want to investigate the number of letters in first names.

   a) What question do you need to ask?

   b) Carry out this investigation on 20 people and present your findings as a chart.

2 You decide to extend your investigation to test whether there are more letters in girls' names than boys' names.

   a) What extra information would you need to collect?

   b) Repeat the investigation, and give your answer to the question: which names are longer – girls or boys?

Using and Applying

1 Decide on a survey to answer some questions that you have. Do the survey and present your findings.

2 Look at the results of a friend's survey and suggest other questions that could be asked about their data.

29 More problem solving

What do you need to know?

- How to solve problems involving the four operations

What will you learn?

- How to choose appropriate calculations to solve problems

Example

The word 'change' tells us that subtraction is needed.

Jill's shopping is £4.29. She decides to pay with a £10 note. How much change should she get?

There are only two numbers: 4.29 and 10 and the units are money: £ and p

To get the 'right' answer, subtract the smaller number from the bigger number.

Key facts

All the information you need is written in the question. Read it carefully. To be sure, read it twice or even three times.
The words in a problem tell you which operation to use.

ADD	SUBTRACT	MULTIPLY	DIVIDE
total	how much change	times	share
altogether	how many more	double	half
sum	how many less	twice	one-tenth

Then decide which numbers to use. Order doesn't matter with adding and multiplying, but it does when subtracting or dividing.

Language

Problem solving means working out what to do to find the answer to a question.

On Track

1 A piece of rope 214cm long is cut into four equal pieces.
Which sum gives the length of each piece in centimetres?
a) 214 ÷ 4   **b)** 4 ÷ 214   **c)** 214 – 4   **d)** 214 + 4

2 It takes Carol four minutes to wash a window. She wants to know how long it will take to wash eight windows. What calculation should she do?
a) 8 ÷ 4   **b)** 8 + 4   **c)** 8 – 4   **d)** 8 × 4

Aiming Higher

1 Make up a problem that will need you to use division to solve it.
What words will you use to show that division is necessary?

2 Make up a problem that will need you to use subtraction to solve it.
What words will you use to show that subtraction is necessary?

3 Swap your problems for questions 1 and 2 with a friend and solve them.
Check your friend's working.

Using and Applying

1 Consider this problem: Jill's shopping is £4.29. She decides to pay with a £10 note. How much change should she get?
a) Explain what calculation you need to make to solve this problem.
b) Do the calculation, being careful to lay out your working well, and write the answer to the problem as a sentence.

2 Consider this problem: Jemima buys two coconuts and half a kilo of bananas.
Explain what you need to make to calculate how much Jemima spends altogether.
Do the calculation, showing all your working, and write your answer as a sentence.

coconuts
78p each

bananas
£1.20 for 1 kg

Glossary

a.m.   stands for ante meridiem – before midday

acute   less than a right angle

analogue clock   uses hands on a clockface dial, rotating to show the time passing

array   a rectangular arrangement

centi   means one-hundredth part

denominator   the number on the bottom of a fraction

digital clock   uses digits (not a dial and hands) to show the time to the nearest minute

frequency   the number of times something happens

horizontal   a line that follows the horizon

kilo   means one thousand times

leap year   happens every fourth year, when the year is exactly divisible by 4, except for years ending with '00', when they must be exactly divisible by 400

milli   means one-thousandth part

numerator   the number on the top of a fraction

obtuse   greater than a right angle but less than two right angles

p.m.   stands for post meridiem – after midday

parallel   lines that remain the same distance apart

partition   to split a number, for example, into Ts (tens) and Us (ones)

perpendicular   at right angles

perimeter   the total distance along the sides of a shape

place value   the value of a digit due to its position within a number

vertical   at right angles to the horizontal